D1092486

HOW TO WIPE OUT YOUR STUDENT LOANS AND BE DEBT FREE FAST:

Everything You Need to Know Explained Simply

BY MARTHA MAEDA

HOW TO WIPE OUT YOUR STUDENT LOANS AND BE DEBT FREE FAST: EVERYTHING YOU NEED TO KNOW EXPLAINED SIMPLY

Copyright © 2009 Atlantic Publishing Group, Inc.
1405 SW 6th Avenue • Ocala, Florida 34471 • Phone 800-814-1132 • Fax 352-622-1875
Web site: www.atlantic-pub.com • E-mail: sales@atlantic-pub.com
SAN Number: 268-1250

ISBN-13: 978-1-60138-216-0   ISBN-10: 1-60138-216-2

Library of Congress Cataloging-in-Publication Data

Maeda, Martha, 1953-
 How to wipe out your student loans and be debt free fast : everything you need to know explained simply / by Martha Maeda.
     p. cm.
Includes bibliographical references and index.
ISBN-13: 978-1-60138-216-0 (alk. paper)
ISBN-10: 1-60138-216-2 (alk. paper)
1. Student loans--United States. 2. Finance, Personal--United States. I. Title.
LB2340.2.M34 2009
371.2'240973--dc22
                            2008031381

Printed in the United States

PROJECT MANAGER: Melissa Peterson • mpeterson@atlantic-pub.com
INTERIOR DESIGN: Holly Marie Gibbs • hgibbs@atlantic-pub.com
COVER DESIGN: Holly Marie Gibbs • hgibbs@atlantic-pub.com

Printed on Recycled Paper

We recently lost our beloved pet "Bear," who was not only our best and dearest friend but also the "Vice President of Sunshine" here at Atlantic Publishing. He did not receive a salary but worked tirelessly 24 hours a day to please his parents. Bear was a rescue dog that turned around and showered myself, my wife Sherri, his grandparents

Jean, Bob and Nancy and every person and animal he met (maybe not rabbits) with friendship and love. He made a lot of people smile every day.

We wanted you to know that a portion of the profits of this book will be donated to The Humane Society of the United States. *–Douglas & Sherri Brown*

The human-animal bond is as old as human history. We cherish our animal companions for their unconditional affection and acceptance. We feel a thrill when we glimpse wild creatures in their natural habitat or in our own backyard.

Unfortunately, the human-animal bond has at times been weakened. Humans have exploited some animal species to the point of extinction.

The Humane Society of the United States makes a difference in the lives of animals here at home and worldwide. The HSUS is dedicated to creating a world where our relationship with animals is guided by compassion. We seek a truly humane society in which animals are respected for their intrinsic value, and where the human-animal bond is strong.

Want to help animals? We have plenty of suggestions. Adopt a pet from a local shelter, join The Humane Society and be a part of our work to help companion animals and wildlife. You will be funding our educational, legislative, investigative and outreach projects in the U.S. and across the globe.

Or perhaps you'd like to make a memorial donation in honor of a pet, friend or relative? You can through our Kindred Spirits program. And if you'd like to contribute in a more structured way, our Planned Giving Office has suggestions about estate planning, annuities, and even gifts of stock that avoid capital gains taxes.

Maybe you have land that you would like to preserve as a lasting habitat for wildlife. Our Wildlife Land Trust can help you. Perhaps the land you want to share is a backyard— that's enough. Our Urban Wildlife Sanctuary Program will show you how to create a habitat for your wild neighbors.

So you see, it's easy to help animals. And The HSUS is here to help.

THE HUMANE SOCIETY
OF THE UNITED STATES.

2100 L Street NW • Washington, DC 20037 • 202-452-1100
www.hsus.org

DEDICATION

This book is dedicated to my three hard-working daughters and to all the other young students who are committed to making this world a better place for all of us.

TABLE OF CONTENTS

Chapter 9: Setting Goals and Priorities   89

Chapter 10: Choosing a Student Loan Repayment Plan   105

Chapter 11: Managing Your Loan Payments 119

Chapter 12: Getting Someone Else to Pay Off Your Loans 139

Chapter 13: Finding a Good Job   161

Chapter 14: Making a
Budget and Sticking to It   171

Chapter 15: Making the
Most of Your Money   183

Chapter 20: Student Loans and Taxes — 257

Chapter 21: Quick Tips for Paying Off Your Student Loans Fast — 263

APPENDIX A: Creating a Repayment Plan — 265

INTRODUCTION

Congratulations. After years of hard work, you have finally walked across the stage, grasped your diploma, and had your photo taken in a cap and gown. Today is "the first day of the rest of your life." Unlike some of your acquaintances, however, whose families were able to start saving up for their education the day they were born, or who were so brilliant or meritorious that they received a full scholarship, you are walking out into the world burdened with debt. You are among the 65 percent of American college students who are starting their adult lives owing thousands of dollars in student loans. You may feel worried, hopeless, or even depressed, but you should not. You have just accomplished a lifetime achievement. In spite of difficult and even prohibitive financial circumstances, you have acquired a higher education. Now you are about to begin learning some new lessons, lessons that will equip you to make the most of every opportunity and give you the skills you need to realize your highest goals.

You will not be able to pay off your student loans overnight, unless you have a rare stroke of luck. Liberating yourself from debt is a steady process that occurs step-by-step, over an extended period of time. It involves internalizing two basic principles: minimize the amount you have to pay, and make the most of your earning power and your income.

If you are still a student, watching your student loans pile up, this book will help you plan for the future and take advantage of every possible opportunity to lower your interest rates and the amount you will eventually pay. If you are already in default, you will learn the steps that will put you back on the track to good credit and peace of mind.

This book will reveal how to turn a liability into an asset. You will learn how to do each of the following:

- Take control of your finances

- Make the most of what you have

- Set goals

- Look for new opportunities

- Avoid pitfalls

- Manage adversity

You will also learn how to navigate the complexities of student loans and credit card debt, and where to turn for help and information when you need it. You will understand how to develop a positive attitude and appreciate your own value. There is no magic formula that will make debt automatically disappear, there is something better: the discovery that you have the power to direct your own life.

SECTION ONE

UNDERSTANDING STUDENT LOANS

CHAPTER 1

Financing an Education

How Much Does an Education Cost?

According to the College Board's 2007 Trends in College Pricing report, the average annual cost — including tuition, fees, and room and board — of attending a private four-year college in the United States in 2006-2007 was $30,367, and the average annual cost of a public four-year college was $12,796. By the 2007-2008 academic year, costs had risen by approximately 5.9 percent. Based on these averages, four years at a private college will end up costing about $129,000, and four years at a public college, about $54,200. This is not taking into account all the students who spend five or six years at college before graduating with a degree.

It makes economic sense for a modern nation to have a large number of well-educated, highly qualified people in its work force. Education also reduces the number of people living in poverty. Studies indicate that almost all graduating high school students who have the academic qualifications to enter college do go on to get at least some higher education. Most students cannot afford a college education without receiving some kind of financial assistance or taking out a loan. The United States government supports a number of programs that encourage qualified students to get a higher education, including grants and affordable low-interest loans.

Is It Worth the Price?

A 2007 College Board Study, Education Pays, found that graduates with a bachelor's degree earn over 60 percent more than people with only a high school diploma. Over a lifetime, this translates into a difference of more than $800,000. Seen in these terms, a loan taken out to finance a bachelor's degree is a worthwhile investment. Depending on the amount of time it takes to pay off the loan, however, the actual cost of the bachelor's degree may double because of the interest paid. Using the figures above, if a student uses loans to pay one-third of his or her college costs, the total cost of four years at a private college could end up being $214,400 to $257,570, and the total cost of four years at a public college could be $90,340 to $108,400. A bachelor's degree can cost as much as a house.

The benefits of a college degree cannot be measured in financial terms alone. The knowledge and experience gained at school broaden and enrich your mind. Studying with people from different backgrounds and cultures awakens your awareness of the many possibilities that exist in this world. Many college students make lifelong friendships and establish a network of contacts that helps them for decades afterwards.

In a speech during his 2008 presidential campaign, President Obama urged students at the prestigious Wharton School of Business to consider entering a career in public service. A career in which the starting annual salary is $27,000 to $33,000 is not appealing to someone who has just spent $80,000 to earn an MBA. The United States government recognizes that many fields requiring extensive training and expertise, such as healthcare, law enforcement, and teaching, do not offer high salaries to offset the cost of education. Federal and state programs offer student loan forgiveness to borrowers who enter certain types of public service, enlist in the military, or serve in areas of critical need.

Explore All the Possibilities

Borrowing money to pay for a college education should be your last resort. Before taking out student loans, research all the options available to you. You will pay less for an education if you attend a state university in the state where you are a resident. Many states have merit-based and need-based scholarship programs for qualified students. To become eligible, you may need to fulfill requirements such as maintaining a specific grade level in high school, achieving certain scores on SAT or ACT exams, and performing a number of community service hours. Check with your high-school counselor or local school district during your junior year to see what programs are available and how you can qualify. If you are accepted at a private college, you may receive grants or scholarships to help pay for tuition, books, and room and board. In 1998, Princeton University initiated a "no-loan" movement to eliminate loans altogether from the financial aid packages of low-income students. Today, approximately two-fifths of colleges with endowments exceeding one billion dollars have adopted no-loans policies.

Most schools offer a combination of need-based and merit-based scholarships, work study, and federally-insured loans. Work study is a federally subsidized program in which students are paid to work a maximum of 12 hours per week in a job at their college or university. Need-based scholarships require documentation of a student's financial circumstances, usually through the Free Application for Federal Student Aid (FAFSA) supported by the previous year's tax returns for the student and parents. Merit-based scholarships are based on test scores, academic performance, and sometimes a student's field of study or involvement in community service. Each school has a limited amount of funds available for scholarships and grants, and must determine how that money will be distributed. After you have been accepted by a college or university, you will receive an award letter giving the details of the financial aid package offered to you by the school. FinAid.org has two tools — available at **www.finaid.org/fafsa/ awardletters.phtml** — to help you compare award letters from different colleges. The best financial aid package is the one that offers the largest amount in grants or scholarships because these do not have to be paid back — unless you leave school without completing the course of study. Perkins and Subsidized Stafford Loans are both need-based and offer the lowest interest rates and best repayment and forgiveness options.

There may be other ways to subsidize your college education. Many schools give free housing to students employed as Resident Advisors who live in the dormitories and supervise younger students. You may be able to get a stipend if you serve in your school's Student Government Association or in some other official capacity.

College savings plans, called 529 Plans, allow families to set aside tax-free savings to pay for qualified education expenses. Pre-paid College Tuition and Pre-paid College Housing plans in many states lock in current tuition and housing rates when you pay in advance for students who will enter college in the future.

Some employers offer grants, scholarships, or other educational assistance for the children of their employees, particularly if the student is entering a field related to the employer's business. Check whether you or your parents' employer offers education benefits.

After calculating the long-term cost of a student loan, some families may decide it is more prudent to finance at least part of a college education in some other way, such as cashing in bonds, selling stocks, or selling some other asset. Parents may prefer to make regular payments on a low-interest home equity loan than pay a slightly higher interest on a Parental Loan for Undergraduate Studies (PLUS).

Savvy Student Tip:

Don't use an IRA or 401(k) plan to pay for an education. Each family's circumstances are unique. Decisions about funding an education should be made after careful consideration of a family's current situation and future plans. Though parents can withdraw funds from an IRA or 401(k) to pay for education expenses, the future consequences may be serious. Annual contribution limits restrict the amount that can be put back into a tax-deferred account, and a large withdrawal could leave the parents short of funds for their retirement and dependent upon the student in their old age.

Before considering a private student loan, be sure you have received the maximum amount in need-based subsidized federal loans and unsubsidized Stafford loans. Talk to the financial aid office at your school to make sure that you have exhausted all other options. Private loans are not subject to the same government regulation as federally-insured loans and do not offer the same loan forgiveness for death, disability, and public service employment.

CASE STUDY: STUDENT LOANS HELP PAY FOR HIGHER EDUCATION

Tia T. Gordon, Communications and Marketing Consultant, Institute for Higher Education Policy.

The Institute for Higher Education Policy (IHEP) is an independent, nonprofit organization that is dedicated to access and success in postsecondary education around the world. Based in Washington, D.C., IHEP uses unique research and innovative programs to inform key decision makers who shape public policy and support economic and social development.

Co-founded in 1993 by higher education expert and Lumina Foundation for Education President and CEO Jamie P. Merisotis, IHEP offers a nonpartisan perspective through a staff that includes some of the most respected professionals in the fields of public policy and research. It is committed to quality of opportunity for all and helps low-income, minority, and other historically underrepresented populations gain access and achieve success in higher education. This devotion is the major factor for its five areas of focus: Access and Success, Accountability, Diversity, Finance, and Global Impact.

Institute for Higher Education Policy
1320 19th Street, NW, Suite 400
Washington, DC 20036
Tel: (202) 861-8223
Fax: (202) 861-9307

Web site: **www.ihep.org**

"Student loans are an important tool for students to pay for higher education, especially when grant aid alone does not cover tuition and other expenses. It is important for students to understand the benefits and disadvantages of obtaining a

CASE STUDY: STUDENT LOANS HELP PAY FOR HIGHER EDUCATION

loan, as well an estimate of what they will pay after gradua-  tion. For some students, loans are necessary in order to attend college and achieve a degree, and may even be a better choice than working full-time or using other strategies to pay for college. However, there is concern about students who take on too much debt and cannot repay, especially if they drop out without a degree.

"Little research has been done in this area, but our sense is that loan forgiveness programs for teachers and health care providers are underutilized.

"Students have different reasons for attending private institutions and varying abilities to take on private loans. It is important for students and their families to understand how private loans differ from federal student loans, especially in regard to the adjustable rate terms that most private loans include. Clearly, students should maximize federal student loans before turning to private loans. But as with loans in general, it is important that students and families have a plan for repaying a private loan before obtaining one.

"Financial aid offices generally first package the federal and state grants for which a student is eligible. Federal and state aid have requirements that usually cannot be changed except in isolated instances. Financial aid offices also consider whether a student is eligible for institutional aid (grants or scholarships offered by the college itself), and this is where some flexibility may exist.

"Students (and their parents) may not be as well informed as they should when it comes to understanding the entire financial aid process. We recommend that students educate themselves as much as possible to become knowledgeable about what types of financial aid is available to them and, if necessary, how they will manage that debt upon graduating."

Financial Aid

How to Apply for Financial Aid

To apply for financial aid, fill out the Free Application for Federal Student Aid (FAFSA), available on the Federal Student Aid Web site, at **www.fafsa.ed.gov**. You can also request a paper FAFSA by calling the Federal Student Aid Information Center at 1-800-4-

FED-AID (1-800-433-3243) or 1-319-337-5665, or from your high-school guidance counselor. The FAFSA is used to determine your eligibility not only for federal assistance, but for financial aid from your state and school.

Savvy Student Tip:

There is no fee for filling out a FAFSA. You can get assistance by filling it out online, by calling 1-800-4-FED-AID, or from a high-school guidance counselor. Some private businesses pose as government agencies and try to charge a fee for filling out the FAFSA or applying for scholarships. Be wary of any consultant or organization that asks you for money.

A+

SAVVY STUDENT

The FAFSA gathers important information that determines your eligibility for need-based grants and subsidized loans. Information is required for both the student and parents, and includes some data from the previous year's tax returns, such as the Adjusted Gross Income (AGI) and number of dependents. If your tax returns are not available, you can use a worksheet to estimate annual income. A student who is not able to fill in the information on his or her parents' financial status will need to communicate individually with the financial aid department of each school.

Each year, the new FAFSA becomes available on January 15. Fill out your FAFSA as early as possible, so that the information can be transmitted to your school financial aid office. Schools have a limited amount of funds available for financial aid programs, and some are distributed on a first-come first-serve basis.

Savvy Student Tip:

There is a government initiative to make the FAFSA easier by 2010. In January 2008, the House of Representatives passed a bill that would simplify filling out the FAFSA by allowing families to check a box on their tax returns that would automatically transfer their financial data to an electronic FAFSA. During his election campaign, President Obama promised to streamline the application for financial aid by replacing the FAFSA with information from income tax returns.

What to Expect

After you submit a completed FAFSA, the Department of Education will generate your Student Aid Report (SAR) and either send a copy by mail or send you an e-mail telling you how to access it online. A copy of your SAR will be sent to each of the schools you entered on your FAFSA. The SAR may ask you to submit additional information or it may give your Expected Family Contribution (EFC). The EFC is not necessarily what you and your family are expected to pay for your education; it is a calculation used by schools in determining how much you can receive in federal grants, loans, and work-study awards. The formula used to calculate the EFC can be found in Part F of Title IV of the Higher Education Act of 1965, as amended (HEA). Updated worksheets for calculating the EFC are available on the Federal Student Aid Web site, at **http://ifap.ed.gov/ifap/byAwardYear. jsp?type=efcformulaguide**.

If you are asked to submit additional information, do it immediately by selecting "Make Corrections to a Processed FAFSA" on the FAFSA home page, at **www.fafsa.ed.gov**, or by writing the corrections on the SAR and mailing it in. Your school may ask you to "verify" your eligibility for student aid by submitting copies of your tax returns or other documentation.

Each school calculates its annual Cost of Attendance, which includes tuition, fees, room and board, books, and incidentals. The school financial aid office then puts together a financial assistance package of grants, scholarships, work study, and loans to make up the difference between your EFC and the school's Cost of Attendance. Each student is sent an award letter with the details of this package and is given the option of declining or accepting student loans.

Federal Pell Grants

The Federal Pell Grant program, which can be researched further online at **www.ed.gov/programs/fpg/index.html**, promotes access to higher education for low-income students enrolled at least half-time at any of approximately 5,400 institutions. It is offered to undergraduates and to some graduate students studying for advanced degrees in education. The amount of the grant is based on the student's SAR and the school's Cost of Attendance. It is awarded directly through the school and must be distributed in at least two annual amounts. The Pell Grant does not have to be paid back.

State Financial Aid Programs

Each state has some type of financial aid for state residents attending institutions of higher education. States also use the SAR and information from the FAFSA to determine need. High-school counselors and financial-aid offices at qualifying schools typically assist students in applying for state financial-aid programs. A list of state higher-education agencies can be found on the U.S. Department of Education Web site, at **http://wdcrobcolp01.ed.gov/ Programs/EROD/org_list.cfm?category_ID=SHE**.

Scholarships

Billions of dollars in scholarships are available to students entering college, postgraduate study, and vocational institutions. Individual schools have endowments and funds that support their enrollment objectives by offering scholarships to qualified candidates based on merit and need. Employers offer scholarships for employees and their children, and for students specializing in particular fields of study. Scholarships are also available through local and national organizations and as part of public relations initiatives. Ask your high-school counselor or your college academic advisor about applying for school-related scholarships. **FastWeb.com**, a Monster® company, matches student test scores and aptitudes with thousands of possible scholarships. **ScholarshipExperts.com** continually updates its scholarship search. CareerOneStop, an employment Web site sponsored by the U.S. Department of Labor offers a database of more than 5,000 scholarships; you can check it out at **www.acinet.org/acinet/scholarshipsearch/scholarshipresults.asp**.

CHAPTER 2

What Are Student Loans?

Make It Your Business to Know

Student loans are a valuable financial tool. A borrower can use them to buy an education now and pay for it later, when he or she has a degree or professional certification and is earning a higher income. Student loans are available to students of all ages, but they are particularly significant for young high-school graduates who are ready to enter college but do not have financial resources to do so. A financial counselor looking at the "whole picture" of a person's financial biography can appreciate the low interest rates and flexible repayment options offered by student loans. Most student borrowers do not think of student loans as part of an overall financial strategy that will impact the rest of their lives.

When you applied for your student loans, there were likely many things on your mind besides how you were going to pay them off or what being in debt might mean for your future. You were likely just excited and relieved when your application was approved, and preoccupied with registering for the right classes and finding a place to live. When you left school, you were concerned about finding a job, moving, and keeping in touch with your friends and family; arranging your loan payments was low on your list of priorities. However, a student loan is a serious debt obligation. If you manage it poorly, you may end up adding thousands of dollars to your debt, and the damage to your credit rating will have a negative effect on many aspects of your life, including your eligibility for certain jobs, how much you pay for a mortgage, your car payments, and your ability to achieve financial freedom.

Your lender, guarantor, and the U.S. government are interested in ensuring that you will be able to meet your payment obligations. They offer a menu of options to help you achieve a stable financial future, including flexible repayment plans, advice and counseling, and vast quantities of information. It is up to you to take advantage of these resources and gain a clear understanding of what your student loans entail and what is expected of you. Do not remain in the dark. Keep asking until all your questions are answered. In many cases, the answers are not complicated. This section will explain the basics of student loans, where to find information, and how to ask questions.

CASE STUDY: FINAID.ORG IS A VALUABLE RESOURCE FOR STUDENT LOAN INFORMATION

Mark Kantrowitz Publisher, FinAid, Director of Advanced Projects, FastWeb

Mark Kantrowitz is a leading authority on student financial aid and an advocate for access to higher education.

FinAid.org is the leading free source for clear, objective student financial aid information, advice, and tools. FinAid tends to be encyclopedic and includes valuable resources for managing student loans, including:

CASE STUDY: FINAID.ORG IS A VALUABLE RESOURCE FOR STUDENT LOAN INFORMATION

Calculators (**www.finaid.org/calculators**)

– Loan Payment Calculator

– Calculators for the various repayment plans (income-contingent repayment, income-sensitive repayment, income-based repayment, graduated repayment, loan consolidation)

– Student loan advisors (use your likely starting salary to determine how much you can afford to borrow)

– Economic hardship deferment calculator, prepayment calculator, and a dozen other calculators.

The Loans section of FinAid (**www.finaid.org/loans**) includes, among other topics:

– Advice on choosing a lender

– Information about student loans, parent loans, and private student loans

– Consolidation loans

– Defaulting on student loans

– List of education lenders, including the largest education lenders

– Collection agencies

– Secondary markets

– Loan services

– Loan forgiveness

– Current and historical interest rates and loan limits

– Various repayment plans, including extended repayment and income-based repayment

What is a Student Loan?

A student loan is money that is borrowed to pay for school tuition, room and board, and other expenses incurred while studying at an institution of higher learning. Unlike scholarships and grants, student loans must be paid back, with interest.

The three major types of student loans are guaranteed and sometimes subsidized by the government; they include Stafford, Perkins, and PLUS loans, which are taken out and repaid by the student's family. Banks also offer private student loans. Consolidation loans enable a borrower to pay off several individual loans and assume a single monthly payment. Peer-to-peer loans are a recent innovation in which a student signs a formal loan contract to borrow money from a friend or family member for education expenses.

According to the 2003-2004 *National Postsecondary Student Aid Study* (NPSAS), two-thirds (65.7 percent) of four-year undergraduate students graduated with some debt, and the average student loan debt among graduating seniors was $19,237 — including Stafford, Perkins, state, college, and private loans but excluding PLUS loans. Approximately 10.8 percent of parents borrowed PLUS loans for their children's college education, with a cumulative PLUS loan debt of $16,317. *Student Debt and the Class of 2007*, an annual report by the Project on Student Debt, estimated that in 2007, student borrowers in private colleges graduated with an average student loan debt of $25,700, and student borrowers who attended public universities graduated with an average debt of $19,400.

Unfortunately, approximately half of the freshmen who enter postsecondary institutions in the United States do not graduate with a degree. According to *Enrollment in Postsecondary Institutions, Fall 2006*, a report compiled by the Institute of Education Sciences of the U.S. Department of Education, only 50 percent of all students pursuing a bachelor's degree graduated within four years from private not-for-profit institutions, 29 percent graduated within four years from public institutions, and only 26 percent graduated within four years from private, for-profit institutions.

In *A Matter of Degrees: Improving Graduation Rates in Four-Year Colleges and Universities (2004)*, the Education Trust reported that almost half of all first-time college students do not graduate within six years. While some of these students eventually complete their studies, many young people leave school owing a large amount in student loans, but without the benefit that a college degree provides in finding employment.

Savvy Student Tip:

The implications of student loan debt for the national economy are serious. Not only are students' parents embroiled in consumer debt and mortgage obligations, but young people are entering the work force today carrying a substantial debt that must be paid off in, addition to putting aside savings to purchase a home or invest in a retirement account. This debt impacts the discretionary spending that fuels economic growth and limits individuals' ability to afford essential healthcare and insurance.

History of Student Loans

History of the Student Loan in the United States

The first student loan program began at Harvard University in 1840. During the 1930s, various programs were established to assist students financially, such as the Indiana Student Financial Aid Association — the first state financial aid association — and the National Youth Administration to provide employment for college students in 1935; and a Public Health Service fellowship program in 1937. The G.I. Bill — *Servicemen's Readjustment Act of 1944* — signaled a new form of government involvement in providing financial assistance to students and recognized the connection between higher education and increased economic productivity.

World War II veterans were guaranteed one year of education for ninety days of service, and one month of education for every month of active service, up to a maximum of forty-eight months. Approximately 51 percent of servicemen took advantage of this opportunity, and the government added the College Scholarship Service, a forerunner of National Defense Student Loans, which later became the Perkins loan program.

During the 1950s, a number of fundamental principles and procedures were formalized under the College Scholarship Service (CSS), an association of colleges, universities, and other educational organizations founded in 1954 to promote college success and opportunity for students. The CSS, now the financial aid division of the College Board, compiles financial data from students and reports it to more than 600 colleges, universities, and graduate and professional schools who use it to determine the financial aid needs of student applicants. The CSS firmly established the concept of need-based aid, and its policies influenced the development of government-subsidized assistance to students. Research conducted by the CSS suggested that while need-based grants would provide access to higher education, need-based loans would help to expand students' choice of educational institutions and opportunities.

Higher Education Act of 1965

The *Higher Education Act of 1965* (Pub. L. No. 89-329) (the "HSA"), part of President Lyndon Johnson's "Great Society" domestic initiative, increased the amount of federal money given to universities, created scholarships, established a National Teachers Corps, and provided for federally-insured, low-interest loans for students with the Federal Family Education Loan Program (FFELP), also known as the Guaranteed Student Loan (GSL) Program — forerunner of the Stafford Loan Program. To encourage banks to join the program and make loans to students, Congress agreed to guarantee a large percentage of any losses.

The *Higher Education Act of 1965* was reauthorized in 1968, 1972, 1976, 1980, 1986, 1992, 1998, and 2008. Each reauthorization introduced modifications and new initiatives, many of which are incorporated in today's student loans. Programs were also modified several times when Congress passed measures to reduce government spending that included cuts to student aid programs. The most recent authorization for the programs in the *Higher Education Act* expires at the end of 2013.

In 1972, the Student Loan Marketing Association — Sallie Mae — was established to create a secondary market for guaranteed student loans. The Education Amendments of 1976 (*PL94-482, Reauthorization of the Higher Education Act*) added state loan-guarantee agencies. In 1978, the *Middle Income Student Assistance Act* expanded eligibility for the Basic Education Opportunity Grant (BEOG) — the Pell Grant — to include middle-income students and eliminated income restrictions for GSL loans. The *1980 Reauthorization of the Higher Education Act* established PLUS loans. BEOG were re-named "Pell Grants," after Senator Claiborne Pell of Rhode Island.

The *Omnibus Budget Reconciliation Act of 1981* tied federal student loans to financial need again and added a loan origination fee. The *Student Loan Consolidation and Technical Amendments Act of 1983* set the interest rate for Guaranteed Student Loans at 8 percent. The 1986 reauthorization of the *Higher Education Act* required students to demonstrate financial need to qualify for the GSL interest subsidy; renamed the NDSL as "Perkins Loan;" created Supplemental Loan to Students (SLS) for graduate, professional, and independent students; limited PLUS loans to parent borrowers; and introduced the Family Federal Education Loan (FFEL) program consolidation loans. The GSL Program was renamed the "Stafford Loan Program" in 1987. In 1988, Congress passed a *Supplemental Loans to Students Reform Bill*, and in 1989, the *Student Loans Reconciliation Amendments*.

Several changes introduced by the *Higher Education Amendments of 1992* led to a steady decline in national student loan default rates. The length of time before a delinquent borrower is declared to be in default was increased from 180 days to 270 days; interest rates were reduced; and any college with a default rate of 25 percent or more for three consecutive years — or 40 percent or more in a single year — was eliminated from participation in federal student loan programs. The *1992 Amendments* also added a Direct Lending pilot project and unsubsidized Stafford loans. It eliminated PLUS loan limits so that families could borrow as much as the entire cost of a college education.

The *1993 Student Loan Reform Act* created direct lending and income-contingent repayment. In 1993, the *National Service Trust Act* (AmeriCorps) established education grants for students aged 17 and older who perform community service. The *Taxpayer Relief Act* of 1997 introduced a tax deduction for up to $2,500 in student loan interest. The *Higher Education Amendments of 1998* added Extended Repayment, reduced Stafford loan interest rates by 0.8 percent, changed the way in which the interest rate for consolidated loans was calculated, and established a loan cancellation program for teachers. Financial aid administrators now had the authority to refuse certification of individual student loan applications, as long as the school did not discriminate based on race, national origin, religion, sex, marital status, age, or disability status.

In 1999, Direct Lending introduced Direct Loan discounts — a 1 percent reduction in origination fees and 0.25 percent interest rate reduction for signing up for auto debit — to compete with loan discounts offered by FFEL program lenders. The Education Department believed that these concessions would save the government money by preventing defaults and would reduce costs for students. Public Law 107-139 (February 8, 2002) replaced variable education loan interest rates with fixed rates for new loans issued after July 1, 2006: 6.8 percent on Stafford Loans and 7.9 percent on PLUS Loans.

The *Higher Education Reconciliation Act of 2005 (HERA 2005)*, part of the *Deficit Reduction Act of 2005* that was narrowly passed by Congress in December 2005, cut $12.7 billion from the student loan programs — the largest reduction in student financial aid programs ever. It included measures that would ordinarily have been included in HERA reauthorization, including higher loan limits for many students and an increase in the number of low-income students who would automatically qualify for the maximum Pell grant. It raised the fixed interest rate on PLUS loans to 8.5 percent and made them available to graduate and professional students.

In 2005, the U.S. Bankruptcy code was amended to exclude "qualified education loans" from discharge during personal bankruptcy proceedings. It also repealed the "single holder rule" that required borrowers whose loans were all held by a single lender to consolidate their loans with that lender, allowing borrowers to consolidate their loans with any lender.

Allegations by the New York Attorney General in 2007 that colleges and universities were receiving payments and referral fees for steering students to specific lenders resulted in the largest education lenders making multi-million-dollar settlements. A new code of conduct was instituted for lenders and colleges, banning certain practices.

The College Cost Reduction and Access Act

Significant changes were made to federal financial aid by the *College Cost Reduction and Access Act (CCRA)*, a budget reconciliation bill signed into law on September 27, 2007. It aimed to reduce subsidies to lenders and guarantee agencies by $19 billion and instead, spend those funds for programs that increase the amounts of student grants, make student loans accessible to more people, reduce interest rates on subsidized Stafford undergraduate student loans by half by 2011-12, allow students to partially repay loans through employment or service in areas of national need, and give colleges incentives for lowering costs to students.

The CCRA limited loan repayment amounts to 15 percent of an individual's discretionary income. It also introduced a pilot auction to set the lender subsidy rates on Parent PLUS loans and addressed problematic practices in the lending industry.

To avert a crisis in the FFEL program, Congress passed the *Ensuring Continued Access to Student Loans Act of 2008* (P.L. 110-227), known as ECASLA, allowing the U.S. Department of Education to purchase unencumbered Stafford and PLUS loans originated between 10/1/03 and 9/30/09. It also raised the annual and aggregate loan limits on the unsubsidized undergraduate Stafford student loans and permitted parents to defer repayment on the Parent PLUS loan until six months after the student leaves school.

After more than a dozen extension acts, the *Higher Education Act of 1965* was finally reauthorized by Congress in 2008. The *Higher Education Opportunity Act of 2008* (PL 110-315) added numerous new disclosure requirements for lenders, including the *Student Loan Sunshine Act*. It also expanded the time period used to calculate the cohort default rate from two to three years. Education lenders were mandated to report repayment status information to all national consumer credit reporting agencies.

The new Act established three new loan forgiveness programs — Loan Forgiveness for Service in Areas of National Need, a program providing for $5,000 in loan forgiveness to be distributed over a five-year period to borrowers employed in low-paid public service jobs; Perkins Loan Cancellatgino for Public Service; and an income-based repayment plan that ties payment amounts to income and forgives student loans after 25 years if a borrower has consistently experienced economic hardship.

Anatomy of a Student Loan

The federal student loan program is intended to help students pay for higher education by lending them money at interest rates lower than commercial interest rates, with flexible repayment plans that make student loans manageable for young graduates entering the work force. The U.S. government promotes its national interests through loan forgiveness programs that encourage young people to become teachers, health service workers, and public servants. Through the student loan program, qualified students can get a higher education and bear most of the expense themselves, rather than relying on taxpayers to pay for it.

In an ordinary market, a high-school graduate with little or no credit history would not be able to qualify for a loan from a commercial lender, or would be charged extremely high interest rates to compensate for the risk. The federal government makes low-interest student loans possible by transferring that risk to itself, and by giving lenders a guaranteed rate of return.

Where the Money Comes From

The major federal loan programs — Stafford (both Subsidized and Unsubsidized), PLUS, Grad PLUS, and Consolidation — are administered in two ways, the Direct Loan program and the FFEL program. Each college or university decides which program will provide federally guaranteed loans to its students.

The government itself is the lender under the Direct Loan program. The U.S. government borrows money from the U.S. Treasury and disburses it directly to student borrowers through their school financial aid offices. Students repay the loans directly to the government. The Direct Loan program is administered by the U.S. Department of Education, but the federal government hires private contractors to do most of the work of servicing the loans and collecting on defaulted loans.

Under the FFEL program, the government pays subsidies to for-profit and non-profit lenders such as Sallie Mae and *ALL* Student

Loans that remove almost all the risk from student loans. If a federal student loan is not repaid by the borrower, the government pays the lender 97 percent of the outstanding principal and all the interest that has accrued on the loan. This effectively reduces the default risk for the lender to only 3 percent. The government also pays lenders a subsidy called a Special Allowance Payment (SAP) to make up the difference between the fixed 6.8 percent interest rate paid by student loan borrowers and the prevailing short-term market interest rate. When the market interest rate is lower than the fixed interest rate paid by borrowers, the lenders must pass the extra interest on to the government.

Banks and financial institutions do not receive government subsidies for private student loans, and they are not insured against default by the federal government. Many private student loans are marketed through the same lenders that offer federally guaranteed loans. Unlike federally guaranteed loans, private loans have variable interest rates based on the credit rating of the student borrower or cosigner.

The Major Players

The **Government of the United States** creates and monitors legislation governing student loans, appropriates funds for student loan and loan forgiveness programs, and borrows funds from the U.S. Treasury to lend directly to students through the Direct Loan program.

The **U.S. Department of Education** administers student loan and financial aid programs (including the FAFSA and SARs), reimburses guarantors who have paid back defaulted loans, makes Special Allowance Payments (SAPs) to lenders, and, in some cases, takes on responsibility for collecting on defaulted loans.

For-profit and non-profit lenders supply the funds for student loans under the FFEL program. Loan funds may come from investors and banks and financial institutions or from the issuing of bonds. Lenders are protected from risk by the U.S. government. They may service the loans directly or contract with loan servicing companies to collect payments and work with student borrowers.

Guarantors predate the FFEL program and act as student loan insurers and administrators. There are currently 34 active guaranty agencies of various types. They reimburse private lenders for their losses when student loans go into default, act as a collection service for the federal government, assist borrowers who are having difficulty paying their loans, and, in some cases, act as lenders themselves. Some guaranty agencies also administer state-level loan and financial aid programs.

Investors are the millions of people who place their savings in the hands of banks and financial institutions so that the money can be loaned out and bring in a steady rate of return. They rely on the interest from student funds to grow their retirement savings, pension funds, and their own children's college funds.

Student loans offer lower interest rates and more flexible repayment plans than other loans or lines of credit. They are structured so that a student does not enter repayment until after he or she has left school and had several months to find employment. Deferment and forbearance are available for borrowers who go back to school, enter active military service, or participate in certain public service programs.

Only students, and parents of students, who are enrolled more than half-time at qualified education institutions are eligible for student loans. The amount that a student can receive in federal subsidized and unsubsidized loans is restricted, and private loans stipulate that funds should be used only for education-related expenses.

A tax deduction of up to $2,500 is available for interest paid on qualified student loans.

Savvy Student Tip:

Student loans cannot be discharged in bankruptcy. Unlike other types of personal debt, federal student loans cannot be discharged in bankruptcy. The federal government has the authority to garnish wages, income tax refunds, and social security benefits to repay a defaulted federal student loan. Similar protection from bankruptcy discharge was extended to private student loans in 2005.

SAVVY STUDENT

How to Get a Student Loan

The first step in applying for a student loan is to fill out a FAFSA — see "How to Apply for Financial Aid" in Chapter 1. On the application, list the schools to which you have applied. Based on your FAFSA, the Department of Education will prepare a SAR, which the schools will use to determine how much you are eligible to receive in Perkins and Subsidized and Unsubsidized Stafford loans. The school will also offer PLUS loans to make up the difference between its Cost of Attendance and the amount available in financial aid. The school will ask you to sign a Master Promissory Note, and the federal loan funds will be disbursed through the school financial aid office. Loans are disbursed in at least two installments, none of which can exceed half of the total amount of the loan. The funds will be applied to tuition, fees, room and board, and other charges payable to the school, and a check will be issued to the student for the remaining balance of the loan.

Savvy Student Tip:

Loans for first-time borrowers are not disbursed for 30 days. If you are a first-time borrower and a first-year undergraduate, the school often cannot disburse your first loan installment until 30 days after the beginning of enrollment. This is to protect you from having a loan to repay if you do not start classes or drop out in the first month. Most schools will waive tuition and room and board until the loan is disbursed and even issue vouchers allowing students to purchase books and supplies in the campus bookstore.

A+
SAVVY STUDENT

Parents may not qualify for PLUS loans because they are not creditworthy, or they may not be able to immediately begin making the required monthly loan payments. If you are still short of necessary funds after your financial aid and student loan options have been exhausted, you can apply for private student loans. The school may recommend a private lender that is serving other students at the school, or you can apply directly to a student lender like Sallie Mae, online at **www.salliemae.com**. Once your application has been approved, you must choose a bank or lender. You will be asked to sign and mail in a promissory note.

You can also shop for student loans directly from banks and credit unions, or through comparison Web sites like **eStudentLoan.com** or **FindStudentLoans.com**. Private loans may be difficult to compare because of their varying APRs, fees, and repayment terms. **FinAid.org** offers a Loan Discount Analyzer at **www.finaid.org/**

calculators/loandiscountanalyzer.phtml that helps convert loan offers into similar terms. If you are having difficulty obtaining a private loan, peer-to-peer lending companies like Greennote.com (**www.greennote.com**) allow you to arrange a formal loan from a private individual.

CHAPTER 3

Government Student Loans

Who gets Government Loans?

Government student loans are guaranteed and subsidized by the U.S. Government. They are typically arranged and disbursed through the school's financial aid office and the funds are applied directly to qualified education expenses, such as tuition, fees, and dormitory costs. Subsidized loans, in which the government pays the interest while the student is in school or in deferment, are based on a student's demonstrated financial need. Unsubsidized loans are available to any student, regardless of need. There is a limit to the amount that can be borrowed each academic term. You cannot qualify for a government loan if you are not a United States citizen or qualified non-citizen (such as a Green Card holder), have a drug conviction, or are eligible but have not registered for Selective Service.

Stafford Loans

Stafford student loans are the most common type of government loan. They are low-interest loans made to undergraduates who attend an accredited college or university as full- or half-time students. Loan payments are deferred while you are in school. The government pays the interest on subsidized Stafford loans during your in-school deferment, but you are responsible for paying the interest that accrues on unsubsidized loans while you are in school. You can either begin making interest payments while you are in school, or allow the interest to be added to the principal balance of the loan when your deferment ends, increasing the size and cost of the loan.

There are two types of Stafford Loans — Federal Family Education Loans (FFEL) and Direct Loans. Private lenders, such as banks, credit unions, savings & loan associations, and non-profit lenders fund FFEL program loans, which are guaranteed against default by the federal government. The U.S. government provides Stafford loans under the William D. Ford Federal Direct Student Loan Program (FDSLP) directly to students and their parents through "Direct Lending Schools." Most schools participate in either the FFEL or Direct Loan program, but some schools participate in both programs. Rules for eligibility and available loan amounts are the same under both programs, but the repayment plans are slightly different.

The amount of subsidized Stafford loans you receive is based on financial need and is determined once you have submitted your FAFSA. According to **StaffordLoan.com**, approximately two-thirds of subsidized Stafford loans are awarded to students with a family Adjusted Gross Income (AGI) of under $50,000, one-fourth to students with a family AGI of $50,000 to $100,000, and a little less than 10 percent to students with a family AGI over $100,000.

Every student is eligible for unsubsidized Stafford loans, but there is a limit on the total amount of Stafford loans a student can receive while studying for a degree. A dependent undergraduate first-year student enrolled in a program of study for at least a full academic year can receive $5,500, for loans first disbursed on or after July 1, 2008. No more than $3,500 of this amount can be in subsidized loans. A dependent student who has completed a first year of study can receive $6,500 if the remainder of the program of study is at least a full academic year, but no more than $4,500 of this can be in subsidized loans. After completing two years of study, the student can receive $7,500 per year if the remainder of the program is at least a full academic year. No more than $5,500 of this amount can be in subsidized loans.

Independent undergraduates and those whose parents do not qualify for a PLUS loan can receive $9,500 the first year — no more than $3,500 of this may be subsidized loans; $10,500 the second year — no more than $4,500 of this may be subsidized loans; and $12,500 the third and fourth years — no more than $5,500 of this amount may be in subsidized loans. Medical students and graduate and professional students can receive additional amounts. All lenders offer the same interest rate for the Stafford Loan, although some give discounts for on-time and electronic payment.

Stafford Loans disbursed before July 1, 2006 had variable interest rates based on the 91-day T-bill rate + 1.7 percent during school with an additional 0.6 percent increase upon graduation, capped at 8.25 percent or less, depending on yearly adjustments. Stafford Loans with a first disbursement after July 1, 2006 now have a fixed interest rate of 6.8 percent.

The interest on subsidized loans first disbursed after July 1, 2008 is fixed at 6.0 percent, with an incremental decrease for loans first disbursed in 2009, 2010, 2011, and 2012. These reductions apply only to subsidized Stafford loans; interest on unsubsidized loans will remain at 6.8 percent.

Perkins Loans

Perkins Loans, formerly known as National Defense Student Loans and National Direct Student Loans, are low-interest loans awarded by a school to undergraduate and graduate students with exceptional financial need. The federal government sets aside a limited pool of money to fund these loans, and the school is expected to make a contribution that is equal to at least one-third of the amount provided by the government. Approximately 1,800 postsecondary institutions offered Perkins Loans in 2008, but the number is expected to increase under the Obama administration. A Perkins Loan offers better terms and benefits than any other student loan. It is a subsidized loan, meaning that the interest is paid by the federal government during the in-school deferment and grace period, which is nine months after graduation instead of the usual six months. Perkins Loans have no origination or default fees. The interest rate is 5 percent, and the loan has a 10-year repayment period.

The school's financial aid office decides the amount of a Perkins Loan. The limit for undergraduate students is $4,000 per academic year, and for graduate students, up to $6,000 per academic year, with a total limit of $20,000 for undergraduate loans and $40,000 for undergraduate and graduate loans combined.

Deferment and forbearance for a Perkins Loan is handled by the school or a servicing agency to which the loan has been assigned. A Perkins Loan has a more favorable cancellation policy than Stafford or PLUS loans. Borrowers of Perkins Loans who undertake certain public service or teaching employment, service in the Peace Corps or ACTION, or active military service qualify to have all or part of their loans canceled. The schools issuing the loans are reimbursed for 100 percent of the principal amount of the canceled loan and must reinvest that reimbursement in the school's revolving loan fund.

Perkins Loans are not eligible for public service loan forgiveness under the *College Cost Reduction and Access Act of 2007*. They can be included in a Federal Direct Consolidation Loan, which is then eligible for public service loan forgiveness. A borrower in a low-paying public service job can use income-based or income-contingent repayment plans to keep monthly loan payments for a Direct Consolidation Loan relatively low until the loan is canceled after ten years of full-time employment.

PLUS Loans

Parental Loans for Undergraduate Students (PLUS) are designed to help parents meet the Expected Family Contribution (EFC) for a dependent undergraduate student enrolled at least half time in an eligible program at an eligible school. Like Stafford loans, PLUS loans are available from lending institutions through the Federal Family Education Loan (FFEL) Program and directly from the federal government through the William D. Ford Federal Direct Loan (Direct Loan) Program. Parents must have an acceptable credit history to qualify for a PLUS loan. The yearly limit on a PLUS Loan is equal to the student's cost of attendance minus any other financial aid received. Any money remaining after tuition, fees, and other charges have been paid is disbursed to the parents and must be used for education expenses. PLUS loans are guaranteed by the federal government. Parents are charged a fee of up to 4 percent of the loan amount, deducted from the disbursement.

PLUS loans disbursed on or after July 1, 2006 have a fixed interest rate of 7.90 percent for Direct PLUS Loans and 8.50 percent for FFEL PLUS Loans. For PLUS Loans disbursed between July 1, 1998 and June 30, 2006, the interest rate is variable and is determined on July 1 of every year. PLUS loans are never subsidized; interest is charged on a PLUS loan from the date of the first disbursement until the loan is paid in full. PLUS loans cannot be consolidated with other student loans, and parents remain responsible for these loans, even if the student later takes over the payments.

Repayment on PLUS loans that are first disbursed on or after July 1, 2008, can begin either 60 days after the loan is fully disbursed or six months after the dependent student ceases to be enrolled on at least a half-time basis. If payment is deferred, interest continues to accrue. Parents can apply for forbearance or deferment of PLUS loans based on their own personal circumstances, not the student's.

HRSA Loans

The Health Resources and Services Administration (HRSA) of the U.S. Department of Health and Human Services offers several need-based loans. To qualify, the borrower must be a citizen, national, or a lawful permanent resident of the United States and must apply through the financial aid office of the school where he or she intends to study.

Nursing Student Loan Program

The Nursing Student Loan program provides long-term, low-interest-rate loans to full-time and half-time students pursuing a course of study leading to a diploma or associate, baccalaureate, or graduate degree in nursing. Schools participating in the plan are responsible for selecting loan recipients and determining the amount of assistance a student requires. The Health Professions Student Loan program provides long-term, low-interest-rate loans to full-time students to pursue a degree in dentistry, optometry, pharmacy, podiatric medicine, or veterinary medicine.

Loans for Disadvantaged Students Program

The Loans for Disadvantaged Students program provides long-term, low-interest-rate loans to full-time students from disadvantaged backgrounds to pursue a degree in allopathic medicine, osteopathic medicine, dentistry, optometry, podiatric medicine, pharmacy, or veterinary medicine. Funds are awarded to accredited schools that are responsible for selecting loan recipients, determining need, and providing loans that do not exceed the cost of attendance, including tuition, reasonable educational expenses, and reasonable living expenses.

Primary Care Loan Program

The Primary Care Loan (PCL) program is a low cost federal loan program for medical students committed to primary health care practice. Borrowers must be full-time students pursuing a degree in allopathic or osteopathic medicine at an accredited school.

Medical students receiving a PCL must agree to enter and complete residency training in family medicine, internal medicine, pediatrics, combined medicine/pediatrics, preventive medicine, or osteopathic general practice within four years after graduation and to practice in primary care for the life of the loan. The interest rate is 5 percent and begins to accrue following a 1-year grace period after the borrower ceases to be a full-time student.

The PCL provides significant savings compared to other federal student loans and offers deferment of principal and interest not available through other loan programs. The maximum award for first- and second-year students is cost of attendance, including tuition, educational expenses, and reasonable living expenses. Loans to third- and fourth-year students may be increased to repay outstanding balances on other loans taken out while in attendance at that school. The primary healthcare service obligation may be waived if the student terminates studies before graduating and does not later resume studies. The outstanding loan balance will be computed annually at an interest rate of 18 percent from the date of noncompliance. Loan repayment periods may be no less than ten years or more than twenty five years, at the discretion of the institution.

Health Education Assistance Loan Program

The Health Education Assistance Loan (HEAL) program provided federal insurance for educational loans made by private lenders to more than 156,000 graduate health professions students between 1978 and 1998. New HEAL loans were discontinued September 30, 1998. Many HEAL borrowers are currently in repayment; as of February 2009, $143,829,589 of HEAL loans was still outstanding.

Types of Student Loans

Type of Loan	Need-based	Restricted Amount	Interest	Interest Rate	Fees	Grace Period	Forbear-ance	Defer-ment	Repay-ment Plans	Pre-payment Penalty	Govt Loan Forgive-ness	Credit Check
Perkins	Yes	Yes	Fixed	5%	No	9 mos.	Yes	Yes	Flexible	No	Yes	No
Stafford Subsidized	Yes	Yes	Paid by government while student is enrolled in school more than half-time, during 6-month grace period and during authorized deferment.	July 1, 2008–June 30, 2009: 6%. July 1, 2009–June 30, 2010: 5.6%. July 1, 2010–June 30, 2011: 4.5%. July 1, 2011–June 30, 2012: 3.4%. After July 1, 2012: 6.8%.	Yes- up to 2%, deducted from disbursements	6 mos.	Yes	Yes	Flexible	No	Yes	No
Stafford Un-susbsidized	No	Yes	Interest accrues while student is enrolled in school more than half-time, during 6-month grace period and during authorized deferment, and is capitalized.	July 1998 - June 2006: Variable, capped at 8.5% After June 2006: 6.8%	Yes- up to 2%, deducted from disbursements	6 mos.	Yes	Yes	Flexible	No	Yes	No
Stafford PLUS Loans	No. Available to parents of dependent children.	Yes	Interest accrues while student is enrolled in school more than half-time, during 6-month grace period and during authorized deferment, and is capitalized.	July 1998 - June 2006: Variable, capped at 9%, currently 5.21% After June 2006: 8.5%	Yes- up to 2%, deducted from disbursements	6 mos.	Yes	Yes	Flexible	No	Yes, if borrower (not student) qualifies.	Yes

Private	No	Typically the cost of attendance minus financial aid	Interest accrues while student is enrolled in school more than half-time, during 6-month grace period and during authorized deferment, and is capitalized.	Variable as spelled out in promissory note, based on borrower's credit rating.	Yes. Fees are capitalized (added to loan balance.)	6 mos.	Depends on the terms of the promissory note.	Depends on the terms of the promissory note.	Depends on the terms of the promissory note.	Depends on the terms of the promissory note.	No	Yes

CHAPTER 4

Private Loans

Private student loans, sometimes called alternative loans, are not subsidized or guaranteed by the federal government, nor are they subject to the same regulation. Private loans are used to make up the difference between available financial aid and federal loans, and what students and families can afford to pay out-of-pocket for college costs. Studies show that 83 percent of undergraduates who take out private loans also have Stafford loans. Students take out private loans when they have reached the Stafford loan limits, or when they are ineligible for federal education loans. Some families are unwilling to fill out the FAF-SA and are attracted by the ease of applying for private student loans. Some families are under the misconception that federal loans are available only to low-income families and that they do not qualify for federal student loans.

Although federal loans still make up the larger percentage of total student loans, the yearly growth of private loans is quickly outpacing federal loans. In 2005-06, the amount of outstanding federal loans was nearly $69 billion, while private student loans amounted to slightly more than $16 billion. By 2006-07 Subsidized Stafford loans had declined from making up 54 percent of all education loans in 1996-97 to 32 percent of all education loans. According to the Institute for Higher Education Policy, some analysts predict that the volume of Stafford loans will grow annually by only 8 percent, while private loan volume will grow by 25 percent annually.

The growth of the private student loan business has been fueled by a number of factors, including a steady and rapid increase in the cost of a college education and the eagerness of banks to loan money to students. Federal grant aid and student loan limits have stagnated while the cost of attending college has risen steadily. Tuition and fees for in-state students at public four year colleges and universities rose 6.6 percent from 2006 to 2007 alone; and increases at private four-year colleges and universities were at least 6 percent. At the same time, federal assistance has shifted away from grants and toward loans. Between 1996-97 and 2006-07, the increase in the amount of money available in federal grants covered, on average, only one-third of the increase in tuition and fees at private colleges, and one-half of the increase at public four-year colleges.

Lenders aggressively market private student loans because federal loan products have become less profitable than they once were. *The Deficit Reduction Act of 2005* and *College Cost Reduction and Access Act* (CCRA) made significant cuts in subsidies for lenders participating in federal loan programs. Many of lenders offering federal student loans also sell private loans and are now expanding into the more lucrative private student loan market. As with other financial products such as credit cards, student loan consolidators, brokers, and companies actively encourage students to borrow private loans by advertising on the Internet and television, through the mail, and by partnering with institutions that offer vocational training and specialized degrees.

Who Issues Private Loans

Most of the lenders in the federal loan program also sell private loans. Some lenders originally developed private loans to provide supplements to their student borrowers of federal loans and to satisfy school requirements for "preferred lenders." As the economic downturn and changes in government educational loan policy have made federal loans less profitable, many of these lenders have begun using their federal loan products to attract borrowers for their private loans. Lenders package both federal and private student loans and sell them as Asset-Based Securities (ABS), mostly to large investors such as financial institutions and pension funds.

Securitized federal and private student loans are typically marketed separately to investors, because the federal loans, which are guaranteed by the U.S. government, are preferred by investors. To make private student loan pools more attractive, most private lenders charge borrowers guarantee fees and purchase insurance with companies such as The Education Resource Institute (TERI) — the oldest and largest private, nonprofit guarantor of private student loans — that ensure that principal and accrued interest will be paid to the lender if the loan goes into default.

A Private Loan versus a Federal Loan

There are important differences between a private and a federal student loan. Private loans are issued by individual banks that set their own lending policies and are not governed by federal guidelines. Private loans are not included in federal loan-cancellation programs, such as Public Service Loan Forgiveness, which means that holders of private loans do not have the same freedom to enter low-paid public service careers. Though they charge higher interest rates than federal student loans, private student loans are similarly protected from discharge during bankruptcy.

Protection

Federal loans offer protections for borrowers, including income-based repayment, deferment, forbearance, and cancellation rights. Private lenders may offer some of these options, but they are not required to. When the lender does offer these options, the details are often not spelled out in the loan document. If a student borrower dies or becomes permanently disabled, a federal loan can be cancelled, but the student's family will still be responsible for paying off private student loans.

Interest Rates

The underlying difference between federal and private loans is that federal loans are structured to benefit the student, while private loans are structured to benefit the lenders and investors. All federal loans have interest-rate caps — in most cases, with fixed rates set at 6.8 percent (8.5 for PLUS loans). Nearly all private loans have variable interest rates with no upper limits, and some have "floors" that limit how low the interest rate can drop. Many private loans are quite expensive, with interest rates of up to 15 percent or higher. The variable rate is often set at the market prime rate plus a "margin" based on the borrower's credit rating. This margin can be as much as 10 percent.

Cost

Private loans are almost always more expensive than federal loans. Except for PLUS loans, borrowers of federal loans are not required to be creditworthy; it is assumed that students have artificially low credit scores because they have little or no credit history. Most private loans are priced according to creditworthiness. A student without a creditworthy cosigner will be charged a higher interest rate because of his or her limited credit history. Some lenders base their rates on the school that a student is attending, charging a higher interest rate for schools with a higher default rate.

Most private lenders charge an origination fee ranging from 2.2 percent to 9 percent. Some charge other fees, such as late payment fees or fees for supplying copies of loan documents.

Not Subsidized

Private loans are never subsidized. Interest starts to accrue as soon as the loan is issued, though payments may be deferred until after graduation. During periods of deferment or forbearance, interest accrues and is capitalized according to the lender's policies.

Default Criteria

Private loans do not have standard criteria for defaults. Borrowers of federal loans are in default when they fail to make payments for a relatively long period of time, usually nine months, or if they fail to meet certain terms of the promissory note. Default conditions for private student loans are specified in the loan contracts, and a private loan may go into default as soon as one payment is missed.

Availability of Information

Information on federal loans can be found on government, school, and financial aid Web sites, in numerous publications, and in school financial aid offices. Data on individual federal student loans is housed in a central database that can be accessed online using your Department of Education PIN number, or by telephone. Information on private loans is supplied by the individual lenders, including Sallie Mae. Some private lenders do not disclose important details about their loans, or they present information in a misleading manner. When you need to know your private loan balance, payment schedule, forbearance options, or any other details, you must contact your lender directly.

Loan Limits

The various federal loan programs are subject to a limit on the amount that can be borrowed. There are no regulations restricting the amount that can be borrowed in private loans. Lenders tend to allow students to borrow up to the cost of attending a school, minus any other financial aid the student has received. Though the loan stipulates that the funds must be used for education expenses, no one is watching over the borrower to enforce this. Sometimes the entire loan is disbursed directly to the student, who then pays education bills. These circumstances contribute to the dangers of over-borrowing or irresponsible spending.

Flexibility

Private loans offer more freedom and flexibility. They can be used to supplement student need and are usually available throughout the year. Private lenders offer loans for nontraditional students and those who might not qualify for a federal loan.

Ease of Application

Borrowers of private loans are not required to fill out the complicated FAFSA and can often apply by completing a simple online form or answering some questions over the phone. Some lenders notify the student right away if the loan has been approved, allowing the student to avoid the uncertainty of a waiting period.

Private Loans and Consolidation

Private loans cannot be consolidated with federal loans. A private consolidation loan can be taken out to pay off federal loans, but this is not advisable because you will no longer qualify for government cancellations and repayment plans.

Savvy Student Tip:

Read the fine print carefully before accepting a private loan. Interest rates, repayment terms, fees, and penalties vary widely among private loans. Read the promissory note carefully before signing.

A Creditworthy Cosigner

Since the interest rate on a private loan is based on the borrower's credit record, you can get a lower interest rate if you find a cosigner for the loan, such as a member of your family. You will get a lower interest rate and lower loan origination fees based on their higher credit score.

Parents who already have a high debt-to-income ratio, or a mother who has a limited credit history because family loans have all been taken out in her husband's name, will probably not qualify to cosign a student loan. Other factors, such as the type of employment, also affect eligibility to be a cosigner. Some lenders require the cosigner to have been employed in his or her current job for 18 months or longer.

The cosigner is equally responsible with the borrower for paying off the loan. If a student defaults or makes irregular payments on a student loan, the cosigner's credit rating is also damaged.

After a borrower has made regular principal and interest payments for a specified period, many private loans allow the borrower to sign a release relieving the cosigner of responsibility while maintaining the original interest rate and terms of the loan.

Savvy Student Tip:

Cosigning a loan is risky. Since many parents have no control over their child's financial transactions after he or she leaves school, cosigning a student loan is risky. The loan may go into default before the cosigner is aware of the borrower's difficulties, and it takes time to repair the resulting negative credit history.

CHAPTER 5

Your Promissory Note

T he promissory note is the contract that you sign with your lender. It is a legal agreement spelling out the terms of your loan, including interest rates, fees, details of repayment, and any legal remedies available to you. It defines your responsibilities as a borrower and authorizes the lender to report your repayment status to credit bureaus, disburse funds to you, and contact you concerning loan payments. The answers to many questions about your student loan can be found in the promissory note. Read it carefully, and report any errors before you sign the note.

When you take out your first Direct Subsidized or Unsubsidized Stafford Loan or FFEL, you will be asked to sign a Master Promissory Note (MPN) that covers all subsequent government loans for the next ten years and contains much of the information in the first section of this book. You can see a sample MPN for Direct Federal Subsidized and Unsubsidized on the Federal Student Aid Web site, at **www.direct.ed.gov/mpn.html**. The MPN asks for your contact information and two references in the United States, followed by a series of authorizations and promises.

It contains detailed information on loan limits, how interest is calculated, cancellation policies, repayment options, procedures for discharge, deferment and forbearance, and charts showing monthly payment amounts and how much will be paid off under each repayment plan. The MPN clearly spells out the legal obligations of the borrower.

The MPN will expire after ten years if the first loan disbursement is not made within twelve months of signing the note or if you notify the lender in writing that you do not wish to use the note for future loans. You may also be asked to sign a new MPN if your school does not participate in the multi-loan program or if you are taking out a loan under a new lender.

CASE STUDY: LEGAL OBLIGATIONS OF A STUDENT LOAN BORROWER

Excerpt from Section C: BORROWER REQUEST, CERTIFICATIONS, AUTHORIZATIONS AND UNDERSTANDINGS of the Master Promissory Note for the Federal Direct Stafford/Ford Loan and the Federal Direct Unsubsidized Stafford/Ford Loan (**http://www.direct.ed.gov/dlmpn.pdf**)

12. Under penalty of perjury, I certify that:

A. The information I have provided on this MPN and as updated by me from time to time is true, complete, and correct to the best of my knowledge and belief and is made in good faith.

B. I will use the proceeds of loans made under this MPN for authorized educational expenses that I incur and I will immediately repay any loan proceeds that cannot be attributed to educational expenses for attendance on at least a half-time basis at the school that certified my loan eligibility.

C. If I owe an overpayment on a Federal Perkins Loan, Federal Pell Grant, Federal Supplemental Educational Opportunity Grant, Academic Competitiveness Grant (ACG), National Science or Mathematics Access to Retain Talent (SMART) Grant, or Leveraging Educational Assistance Partnership Grant, I have made satisfactory arrangements to repay the amount owed.

CASE STUDY: LEGAL OBLIGATIONS OF A STUDENT LOAN BORROWER

D. If I am in default on any loan received under the Federal Perkins Loan Program (including National Direct Student Loans), the William D. Ford Federal Direct Loan (Direct Loan) Program, or the Federal Family Education Loan (FFEL) Program, I have made satisfactory repayment arrangements with the holder to repay the amount owed.

E. If I have been convicted of, or pled nolo contendere (no contest) or guilty to, a crime involving fraud in obtaining funds under title IV of the Higher Education Act of 1965 (HEA), as amended, I have completed the repayment of the funds to the U.S. Department of Education (ED) or to the loan holder in the case of a Title IV federal student loan.

13. For each Direct Subsidized Loan and Direct Unsubsidized Loan I receive under this MPN, I make the following authorizations:

A. I authorize my school to certify my eligibility for the loan.

B. I authorize my school to credit my loan proceeds to my student account at the school.

C. I authorize my school to pay to ED any refund that may be due up to the full amount of the loan.

D. I authorize ED to investigate my credit record and report information about my loan status to persons and organizations permitted by law to receive that information.

E. Unless I notify ED differently, I authorize ED to defer repayment of principal on my loan while I am enrolled at least half time at an eligible school.

F. I authorize my school and ED to release information about my loan to the references on the loan and to members of my immediate family, unless I submit written directions otherwise.

G. I authorize my schools, lenders and guarantors, ED, and their agents to release information about my loan to each other.

H. I authorize my schools, ED, and their respective agents and contractors to contact me regarding my loan request or my loan, including repayment of my loan, at the current or any future number that I provide for my cellular telephone or other wireless device using automated dialing equipment or artificial or prerecorded voice or text messages.

CASE STUDY: LEGAL OBLIGATIONS OF A STUDENT LOAN BORROWER

14. I will be given the opportunity to pay the interest that ED charges during grace, in-school, deferment, forbearance, and other periods as provided under the Act. Unless I pay the interest, I understand that ED may add unpaid interest that is charged on each loan made under this MPN to the principal balance of that loan (this is called "capitalization") at the end of the grace, deferment, forbearance, or other period.

Capitalization will increase the principal balance on my loan and the total amount of interest I must pay.

The Master Promissory Note for Perkins Loans is also effective for ten years after the date of signature, but some schools require borrowers to sign a new promissory note every year. A sample Perkins MPN can be seen on the Federal Student Aid Web site, at **www.ifap.ed.gov/dpcletters/attachments/PerkinsMaster-PromissoryNote.pdf**. It contains important differences from the Stafford MPN, including a nine-month instead of a six-month grace period, and the loan cancellation programs for borrowers employed in certain public service professions.

It is particularly important to review the promissory note for a private student loan — before signing and when the loan is about to enter repayment. Unlike the standard interest rates and repayment terms of federal student loans, those for private loans vary widely. A private loan may go into default after a single payment is missed, and the whole amount of the loan may be payable on the death of the borrower. The method for calculating interest on the loan is explained, and there may be finance charges of as much as 10 percent of the loan principal, and prepayment fees. The promissory note also outlines any forbearance provisions and benefits, such as discounts offered for electronic debit or on-time payments.

CHAPTER 6

Interest

The cost of attendance for a year at a college or university ranges from $13,000 to $40,000, but when you fund your education with student loans, the total cost may be tripled by the time you finish paying it off. Many students would be daunted if they realized how much they are actually paying for their educations. The extra cost is the interest you pay over the life of your loan. Interest is the price you pay for the use of someone else's money. Instead of putting money into a business that might do well some years and slump or even fail in others, someone is investing in you, with confidence that when you graduate, you will earn a good salary and repay not only the amount you borrowed, but a respectable amount of interest for the privilege of using the money. To an investor, your student loan is a commodity guaranteed to provide a steady, predictable income for many years, along with the eventual return of the principal. Since there is always a risk that you will not be able to repay the loan, the loan must be insured, or the interest rate must be high enough to compensate the lender for taking a gamble.

Calculating the exact amount of interest you will pay on your loan is complicated. Each time you make a loan payment, you are paying interest and also paying off a small portion of the loan principal, so that every month, the interest is calculated as a percentage of a slightly smaller amount. If you do not pay interest during periods of deferment or forbearance, it is added to the principal of the loan (capitalized), making the principal larger. It is difficult to know exactly how much you are going to pay for your loan. You can find a number of online calculators that can tell you what you will pay using different repayment plans and paying off your loan over ten, twenty, or thirty years.

Savvy Student Tip:

If your income is limited and you can barely afford your monthly payment, calculating the amount of interest you are going to pay over the next 20 or 30 years is not going to mean much because you have no choice but to pay it. If you have extra money to put into loan payments, knowing how much interest you will pay can help you decide whether to change to a different repayment plan, make extra payments to lower the loan balance, or put some of that extra cash into savings for a mortgage or retirement.

The percentage rate charged for most student loans does not alarm ordinary borrowers because it is expressed as a relatively small number, like 6 or 8 percent. One-sixth of a percent or one-fourth of a percent seems even less significant. When you look at the effect of compounding interest over time, the numbers are alarming, and it is evident that even a fraction of a percent makes a substantial difference in how much you will end up paying. If you look at the chart below, you will understand why it is important to get the lowest possible interest rates on your loans and to do everything in your power to make them even lower. For example, by consolidating your loans during your grace period, you can lower your interest rate .6 percent; over a 30-year repayment period, this would translate into a savings of $1,418 on a $10,000 loan. If you take advantage of a .25 percent decrease in interest by signing up for automatic debit, and another .25 percent decrease for on-time payments, you can save yourself over $300 over 10 years, and over $1,000 over 30 years.

Total Amount Repaid on $10,000, Including Interest

Interest Rate	Original Loan	Interest Paid Over 10 Years	Total Amount Paid Over 10 Years	Interest Paid Over 30 Years	Total Amount Paid Over 30 Years
3.4%	$10000	$1810	$11810	$5966	$15966
4.5%	$10000	$2436	$12436	$8241	$18241
5.0%	$10000	$2728	$12728	$9324	$19324
5.6%	$10000	$3082	$13082	$10440	$20440
6.2%	$10000	$3443	$13443	$12050	$22050
6.8%	$10000	$3809	$13809	$13468	$23468
8.4%	$10000	$4814	$14814	$17424	$27424

Created using the Parent Loan Calculator on CollegeBoard.com
(http://apps.collegeboard.com/fincalc/parpay.jsp)

Suppose you use 12 months of forbearance to delay making the first year of payments on the same $10,000 loan. You do not pay the interest during that period, so it accrues and is added to the loan principal at the end of the year. Over a 30-year repayment period, that year of forbearance could cost you an additional $2,303.

Amount Paid When Interest is Capitalized After One Year of Forbearance:

Interest Rate	Original Loan	Interest Paid Over 10 Years	Total Amount Paid Over 10 Years	Interest Paid Over 30 Years	Total Amount Paid Over 30 Years
3.4%	$10000	$1810	$11810	$5966	$15966
4.5%	$10000	$2436	$12436	$8241	$18241
5.0%	$10000	$2728	$12728	$9324	$19324
5.6%	$10000	$3082	$13082	$10440	$20440
6.2%	$10000	$3443	$13443	$12050	$22050
6.8%	$10000	$3809	$13809	$13468	$23468
8.4%	$10000	$4814	$14814	$17424	$27424

Created using the Cost of Deferment/Forbearance Calculator on CollegeZone.com (http://www.collegezone.com/parentzone/218_2236.htm) and the Parent Loan Calculator on CollegeBoard.com (http://apps.collegeboard.com/fincalc/parpay.jsp)

These calculations do not account for inflation, which causes the dollar to lose buying power over a period of three decades. By the time the loan is paid off, the total amount will have less value in constant dollars than it does today.

Interest Rates on Student Loans:

Interest Rate	Original Loan	Interest Accrued During 1 Year of Forbearance	New Loan Balance	Interest Paid Over 10 Years	Total Amount Paid Over 10 Years	Interest Paid Over 30 Years	Total Amount Paid Over 30 Years
3.4%	$10000	$340	$10340	$1871	$12211	$6169	$16509
4.5%	$10000	$450	$10450	$2546	$12996	$8612	$19062
5.0%	$10000	$500	$10500	$2864	$13364	$9793	$20293
5.6%	$10000	$560	$10560	$3255	$13815	$11263	$21823
6.2%	$10000	$620	$10620	$3656	$14276	$12794	$23414
6.8%	$10000	$680	$10680	$4069	$14749	$14386	$25066
8.4%	$10000	$839	$10839	$5218	$16057	$18888	$29727

These calculations do not account for inflation, which causes the dollar to lose buying power over a period of three decades. By the time the loan is paid off, the total amount will have less value in constant dollars than it does today.

Interest Rates on Student Loans:

Type of Loan	Interest	Interest Rate
Perkins	Paid by government while student is enrolled in school more than half-time, during nine-month grace period, and during authorized deferment.	5%
Stafford Sub-sidized	Paid by government while student is enrolled in school more than half-time, during six-month grace period, and during autho-rized deferment.	July 1, 2008–June 30, 2009: 6%. July 1, 2009–June 30, 2010: 5.6%. July 1, 2010–June 30, 2011: 4.5%. July 1, 2011–June 30, 2012: 3.4%. After July 1, 2012: 6.8%.
Stafford Un-subsidized	Interest accrues while student is enrolled in school more than half-time, during six-month grace period, and during authorized deferment, and is capitalized.	July 1998 - June 2006: Variable, capped at 8.5% After June 2006: 6.8%
Stafford PLUS Loans	Interest accrues while student is enrolled in school more than half-time, during six-month grace period, and during authorized deferment, and is capitalized.	July 1998 - June 2006: Variable, capped at 9%, currently 5.21% After June 2006: 8.5%
Consolidation	Weighted average of the interest rates on loans being consoli-dated, rounded up to the nearest 1/8 of a percent and capped at 8.25%.	
Private	Interest accrues while student is enrolled in school more than half-time, during six-month grace period, and during authorized deferment, and is capitalized.	Variable as set out in promissory note varies according to credit rating.

CASE STUDY: MY INTEREST RATE CHANGED THREE TIMES.

Chris, Age 38, Art Director, Lake Worth, Florida

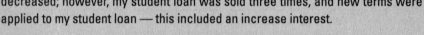

I graduated from college in 1992 from Florida A&M with a bachelor's degree in Journalism & Graphic Communication.

The total loan amount that I had to repay at the time that I graduated was $28,000. I started repaying my student loan by making $350 monthly payments. Each year, my loan amount decreased; however, my student loan was sold three times, and new terms were applied to my student loan — this included an increase interest.

Toward the final year of repaying my student loan, I was paying $100 monthly. I did not make any extra monthly payments outside of what was requested by my lender. I finally paid off my student loan in 2006.

Forbearance, Deferment, and Interest Rates

Capitalization — or the addition of interest to the balance of a loan — after periods of deferment or forbearance, contributes significantly to the amount you ultimately have to pay off. Interest is now calculated based on the new, larger loan balance, and your monthly loan payment becomes larger. Interest that accrues during in-school, grace and deferment periods, and during periods of active military duty is not capitalized until the end of the deferment. If you can make interest payments while you are still in deferment, or a payment just before the end of your grace period or deferment, you can prevent that interest from being capitalized. Interest during periods of forbearance can be capitalized quarterly (every three months) under the Higher Education Act. While you are in forbearance, try to continue making interest payments.

SECTION TWO

Paying Off Your Student Loans

CHAPTER 7

What to Do First

Exit Counseling

To ensure that students understand the responsibilities of repaying their school loans, the federal government requires that all student loan borrowers participate in an exit loan counseling program prior to graduation. The program outlines useful information on the student loan repayment process and requires students to select a repayment option. Further, it offers information on loan consolidation programs and explains what it means to be delinquent or to default on a student loan. It also provides information on various other borrower resources. The Department of Education provides a 30 to 40 minute online exit counseling session for borrowers of Direct Loans (**www.dl.ed.gov/borrower/ CounselingSessions.do?cmd=initializeContext**).

Collect Your Documents in One Place

Your student loan promissory note and the paper statements and notifications that you receive by mail are important legal documents. Sometimes a letter in the mail is the only warning you will receive that you have missed a payment or are about to go into default. That one letter may be sent to fulfill a requirement in your loan contract that the lender notify you before beginning proceedings against you. You may also be entitled to tax deductions on the interest you pay for student loans. Keep the documents for all of your student loans together in a binder or file folder.

If you die or become disabled, your student loans may qualify for discharge, but someone must notify the lender of your situation. Keeping your loan documents in one place will make it easier for your family to know what to do if something unfortunate happens to you.

Mark the Dates on Your Calendar

The repayment period for a student loan begins the day after the grace period expires. PLUS loans enter repayment 60 days after disbursement, unless the borrower has arranged for deferment or forbearance. It is important to be aware of the dates when your first loan payments will become due so that you can plan for them, and to schedule regular payments before the due date each month.

Most lenders now encourage borrowers to make payments online and do not consider a payment late if it is approved on or before the due date, even if it does not actually post to the account until two or three business days later. Lenders give incentives, such as interest rate reductions, to borrowers who schedule automatic debits from their bank accounts, and encourage borrowers to sign up for electronic correspondence so that they can receive notices and statements by e-mail instead of through the regular mail. Payment schedules and histories are often posted online so that the borrower can review them by logging into his or her account.

You can also use the "bill pay" feature of your online bank account to schedule regular payments from your checking account. Set up an e-mail alert to remind you when the payment is about to be debited. Setting up regularly scheduled payments ensures that you do not become delinquent and eliminates stress and worry over due dates.

Keep in Touch

Make sure your lender always has updated contact information for you, including your address, telephone number, and e-mail address. Legal requirements to notify you of delinquent payments or default proceedings are considered satisfied once the notice has been sent to the address on file with the lender or guarantor, regardless of whether you actually receive those notices. If you are using a permanent address, such as your parents' home, make arrangements to have them forward important correspondence to you. Read all the correspondence you receive regarding your student loans, and respond promptly. Recent graduates have a tendency to move around and change addresses frequently, so most lenders now offer incentives for signing up for e-mail correspondence and for setting up regular automated payments from a bank account.

Make Sure You Understand

Review your loan documents and make sure you understand when your first loan payments will become due, how much they will be, what your obligations are, and the repayment options available to you.

Default and Delinquency

A student loan payment is technically delinquent the day after the due date. If you miss one payment, a lender may consider you to be 30 days late even though you believe you are only one day late. If you miss two payments, you may be considered 60 days late, even though only 31 days have passed since the first missed payment. After missing a third payment, you will be considered 90 days late, and the lender may report your delinquency to the credit bureaus.

After you miss a second payment on a government loan, the Department of Education requires the lender to notify the guarantor that you are delinquent and in danger of defaulting on the loan. The guarantor then employs collection specialists to make phone calls and send you warning letters until the loan is brought current through payment, deferral, or forbearance. These procedures are required by law, and neither the lender nor the guarantor can deviate from them.

A government loan (FFEL) scheduled for regular monthly payments can go into default after you have missed payments for 270 days — or 9 months — according to current law. If payments are scheduled less frequently, the loan goes into default after 330 days. Private loans may have different criteria for determining when the loan is in default.

CHAPTER 8

Why You Should Pay Off Your Student Loans Quickly

$15,000 or $45,000

The primary reason why you should pay off your student loans as quickly as possible is the cost of your education. You may have borrowed $15,000 in student loans over four years to pay for tuition, room and board, and the cost of attending a college or university. If you pay off $15,000 in Stafford loans with a fixed interest rate of 6.8 percent over 10 years, you will end up paying $20,715, or an extra $5,715, for your college education. Extend payments over 30 years, and you will have paid an extra $20,202 for your education. (The actual value in constant dollars will be slightly less because of inflation.) That is $20,202 that could have gone toward a down payment on a house or into your savings, where it could grow over time. The sooner you pay off your loan, the less you will have invested in paying for your education. And the earlier you pay down the loan balance, the less interest you will pay over time.

Freedom from Debt

As long as you have a student loan, auto loan, or credit card debt, you have a monthly obligation to make your payments, which means that you need a stable and steady source of income. Being in debt impedes your freedom to try a new career, travel, or handle the risks of launching your own business. You may be willing and able to make personal sacrifices when it comes to food and housing, but you will be obliged to come up with your monthly loan payments, no matter what your circumstances. When you travel to Wyoming to fight wildfires, or to Africa as a freelance journalist, you will need to make arrangements so that your loans do not go into default while you are out of touch. Although you can obtain deferments or forbearance while you do graduate studies, serve in the Peace Corps, or are on active military duty, many other opportunities will not be open to you. In many cases, interest that accrues during periods of deferment is capitalized, adding to the balance of your loan and increasing the total amount that you pay off. Private student loans, which do not have the same repayment and forgiveness options as federal loans, are even more restrictive.

Plan for Your Future

Young graduates may not envision themselves as parents, homeowners, or retirees, but within a few years, many situations will arise that require financial goals and planning. Student loan payments will be joined by other financial obligations, like a mortgage, the expenses of raising a family or caring for elderly parents, and the need to save money for the future. The sooner you pay off your student loan debt, the more money you will have for your other financial objectives. No one enjoys paying for something they have already consumed; almost everyone feels excited when they anticipate future rewards or when they are able to actively invest in the present.

CASE STUDY: I'M GLAD I PAID OFF MY LOAN BEFORE I GOT MARRIED.

Dana, age 36, is a middle school teacher in Wilmington, Delaware.

I graduated from college in 1993 with my bachelor's degree in biology from Shaw University in Raleigh, North Carolina. The original amount of my loan obligation was $10,000 for my undergraduate studies. Later, I returned to school for my master's degree and incurred an additional $7,000 in loans.

When I graduated from college, I began working at a science laboratory. The pay was not very good, so I just paid my requested loan payments. This went on for about a year.

In 1994, I started working for Smith Kline & French Laboratories. The pay was much better, and I was able to pay more than my monthly payment amount — at least $80 more.

I decided to return to school in 1996 to receive my master's degree in Education. The downside to returning to school was that I had to quit my job and complete a student teaching requirement of my graduate program. During that year, I made very little money and was forced to return to making my regular monthly payments. Upon graduation in 1998, I started teaching full-time as a salaried employee and resumed my increased payments. The loan amount decreased significantly with the increased payments, and in 1999, I was able to use my IRS tax return to pay off the remainder of the student loan.

Often, I have contemplated whether I should have saved that extra money for other things, such as a home over an apartment, or a nicer car. However, it was probably the best way to go for me because not long after paying off my loan, I married, and soon after, had my first child. It is not easy to save money when you have a family. Many times, my husband and I find ourselves stretching our finances to pay for private school, extracurricular activities, eyeglasses, and so on. I know

CASE STUDY: I'M GLAD I PAID OFF MY LOAN BEFORE I GOT MARRIED.

that I made the right decision to sacrifice and pay down the loans when I did. If I had not, it would have really affected my new family. Over the years, my family has moved three times to accommodate for its increase in size — which eventually has included three kids, my husband and I, a dog, and a cat.

What Happens If You Do Not Pay?

Consequences of Default

The consequences of a default on a student loan are serious. If you default on a government loan, and the guarantor is unable to rehabilitate the loan, the guarantor must immediately pay the lender the principal and all the interest due on the loan. The guarantor seeks reimbursement from the government, and the government then takes over the job of recovering the loss from you, the borrower.

Once a student loan enters default, rehabilitation is a complicated process, and some of the harmful consequences cannot be reversed. Make use of every option available, including reducing payments and forbearance — explained later — to avoid default.

Seizure of Tax Refunds and Other Benefits

The government has authority to seize federal and state income tax refunds and apply them to your student loan. Instead of receiving a refund check, you will receive a notice stating that your refund has been withheld to repay your student loan. Other federal or state payments may also be withheld. Federal law requires the Department of the Treasury to give you prior notice of the proposed withholding, and an opportunity to review loan records, to demonstrate why the loan is not in default or is not enforceable, and to make arrangements to repay the loan. Guaranty agencies can make arrangements with state governments to withhold state income tax refunds and other payments. The government, guarantor, or lender may take legal action against you in State or Federal District Court. There is no time limit on student loan debt. Even your Social Security payments can be seized if you still have a student loan in default.

Collection Fees

The guarantor has the right to collect up to 25 percent of the original loan balance in collection fees, even if you have made payments for several years and the remaining balance is low. After sending you numerous delinquency notices and warnings, the lender or guarantor will refer your loan to a collection contractor and add the contractor's commission to the amount you owe. You may be responsible for other costs incurred in attempting to collect payment on your loan, including attorney's fees.

Wage Garnishment

If you default on a student loan, the government can implement an administrative wage garnishment without judicial action. Your employer will be required to forward up to 15 percent of your disposable pay directly to the government to repay your loan. This could affect your employment because some employers are reluctant to undertake the extra paperwork, or may consider wage garnishment a sign of fiscal irresponsibility. You can appeal wage garnishment on certain grounds, but you will be required to provide formal documentation to back up all your claims. Some employers will not hire you if you have defaulted on a student loan.

Higher Interest Rates

You may be able to rehabilitate a loan that is in default and begin making regular payments, but the interest rate on your note may be higher, resulting in your paying more for the loan than you would have originally.

Ineligibility for Financial Aid

If your student loan is in default, you may not be eligible to receive financial aid or additional student loans if you decide to return to school to continue your education or get a professional degree. This can be especially harmful if you dropped out of school after one or two years and now wish to return and complete your first degree. Your diploma could be withheld at graduation, or you could lose your professional license. Loans in default are not eligible for deferment or forbearance.

Ineligibility for VA and HUD Loans

If you have student loans in default, you will not be eligible for other types of federal financial assistance, such as mortgages for veterans guaranteed by the U.S. Department of Veteran's Affairs (VA) or various types of home loans insured by the Federal Housing Administration (FHA), a branch of the U.S. Department of Housing and Urban Development (HUD).

Your Credit Score

Lenders are now required to regularly report student loan payment history to the credit bureaus; this includes reporting student loans in default. A default on student loans drastically lowers your credit score and its effect is more difficult to overcome than the effect of declaring personal bankruptcy. A low credit score will determine how much you pay for any future loans, including interest on credit cards and car loans. Some employers look at an applicant's credit scores when hiring for management positions or positions that include responsibility for budgeting or handling money.

CASE STUDY: MY CREDIT RATING SUFFERED BECAUSE I DID NOT UNDERSTAND THE CONSEQUENCES OF NOT MAKING REGULAR PAYMENTS.

Jeanine, Age 38, Charter School Co-Founder, Philadelphia, Pennsylvania

I graduated from college in 1992 with a bachelor's degree in Recreational Management. Because I was part of a Park Rangers program, I had a good portion of my tuition covered. When I graduated, I had close to $10,000 to repay in student loans once the interest was added to the loan. In retrospect, I should have been more consistent with making my student loan payments, as it now does not seem to be as much money as it did to me then.

I paid my student loan very inconsistently during my first year after graduation. I don't know why. I guess I just did not realize the importance of paying it off and what it would do to my credit.

After a year of inconsistent payments, the federal government issued a letter to me informing me that they planned to garnish my employment wages until I had successfully paid off my student loan. The letter said it was due to my lack of consistent payments made on my student loan account.

. I decided not to bother to fight the government because allowing my wages to be garnished was one way to make sure it was paid and to get the debt covered. I did not realize that it would affect my credit at the time. I wish I had…it took a while to rebuild my credit, partly due to the wage garnishment.

CASE STUDY: MY CREDIT RATING SUFFERED BECAUSE I DID NOT UNDERSTAND THE CONSEQUENCES OF NOT MAKING REGULAR PAYMENTS.

For the next seven years, the federal government took a little over $100 from my paycheck — per pay — until my student loan was finally paid off. It was a learning experience, and I am positive that I would have done things differently if I could turn back the clock and begin again after graduation. I plan to attend graduate school eventually. Should I take out a student loan to pay for my education, this experience has taught me the importance of honoring the commitment to repay my bills on time. I now own a home and live very modestly. My credit is very good.

For the next seven years, the federal government took a little over $100 from my paycheck — per pay — until my student loan was finally paid off. It was a learning experience, and I am positive that I would have done things differently if I could turn back the clock and begin again after graduation. I plan to attend graduate school eventually. Should I take out a student loan to pay for my education, this experience has taught me the importance of honoring the commitment to repay my bills on time. I now own a home and live very modestly. My credit is very good.

I would tell anyone with student loans recently graduating from college to be sure to repay their student loans. I would advise them against making my mistake. There are programs to prolong payment if you have a hard time finding a job — like I did in my first year after college. However, it is the responsibility of the student to take charge and seek out services like deferments and forbearances to prevent your credit from begin affected due to inability to keep up with your payments

CHAPTER 9

Setting Goals and Priorities

Take Charge of Your Life

You Have a Choice

Every self-improvement guru will tell you that even if you do not have the power to change your circumstances, you do have the power to change the way you look at them. A setback or a limitation can prevent you from realizing your dreams, or it can be the catalyst that stimulates you to go beyond what you ever thought you could accomplish. You can choose whether to be a victim or a winner. Success is not made up of miracles; just some mental discipline, determination, and effort.

Everything has a cost. Your student loans are a financial obligation, but they are also the price of a better future, of the increased earning potential that you have acquired as a result of your studies, and of the broader mind and greater understanding that you have gained through your college experiences. Do not waste energy on regret and self-doubt; direct your energy toward tackling the situation at hand.

Student loans, unlike other types of loans, are structured to accommodate, to some degree, the economic uncertainties of starting a career and a family. Repayment options allow you to adjust your loan payments to your economic circumstances, at least temporarily. Once you have established yourself in a predictable financial cycle, student loan payments become routine, and the balance gradually diminishes. If you encounter rough spots, you may have to make some changes to manage the difficulties. And if you use extra income to pay off the principal of your loans whenever you can, you will not only emerge from your debt sooner, but you will have lowered the cost of your education.

Only you can take charge of your finances. You cannot expect a bank or a lender to have your best interests at heart. Do not wait for someone else to tell you what to do. Many student loan borrowers end up in default, or pay much more than they need to for their loans, because they do not understand their obligations and are unaware of the resources available to them. Make an effort to find out, for yourself, everything that you need to know. As you become financially literate, you will be able to apply what you have learned to every aspect of your life, and you will be able to help others accomplish their goals.

Do You Know What You Want?

What type of person are you? Do you have a career goal? A mission? A dream? Your life style and your plans for the future will help decide your strategy for paying off your student loans and other debt. Obviously, you cannot pay off a debt without an income. The size of that income, where it comes from, and how you distribute it are determined both by your circumstances and the choices you make. To successfully pay off your debts and mini-mize the amount you lose in interest payments, lost opportunity, late fees, and penalties, a reasonable portion of your income must be set aside to pay off your student loans. You may be able to in-crease the amount of your payments and pay off your loan faster by making a few changes to your life style and sacrificing im-mediate gratification for later rewards. You are the one who will decide which trade-offs are worthwhile.

- Are you hoping to pursue a career in public service? Your salary may be low, but you might qualify for one of the programs that forgive student loans in exchange for a work commitment.

- Do you intend to return to school for a graduate or pro-fessional degree? Your plans should encompass additional student loans, and the possibility of earning income while you study.

- Do you already have a family? Your financial plan will in-clude your partner's contribution, the expenses of caring for children, and possibly a mortgage.

- Are you seeking work experience or training in the field? Consider spending some time in military service or in the Peace Corps.

- Are you an artist, journalist, performer, or writer? Your in-come may fluctuate wildly and unpredictably.

The same strategy is not going to suit everyone, but following some basic principles will ensure success. The following chapters will explain how you can apply these principles and develop an attitude of success.

Visualize the Future

Your self-image is a powerful influence on your thoughts and actions. Begin to picture what you want in your mind — not just in words, but in vivid Technicolor images. Visualize yourself paying off your debt quickly, living a happy, debt-free future. As you identify the steps you will need to take to achieve your goals, add to your library of images with pictures of specific accomplishments: a successful business project, a promotion, a new home, a celebration with friends. Picture yourself doing things you enjoy, strong and in good health, being active, traveling. A clear and positive self-image subconsciously directs your choices and actions toward the fulfillment of your desires.

Make Freedom from Debt a Primary Goal

Make freedom from debt a priority, even if you do not yet see how you are going to accomplish it. Each time you are faced with a decision, evaluate whether the outcome is going to further your goal of paying off your debt and living debt-free. If not, you must decide whether the rewards are worth the amount you will pay in interest by not paying your debt off early. Suppose taking a particular job will give you valuable work experience that will add to your résumé and further your career, but the starting salary is so low that you will have to reduce your payments and pay off your debt over a longer period of time. Is the benefit worth the cost? How about spending your tax refund on a two-week tropical vacation? Are the stress relief and the time spent bonding with your family or friends worth the sacrifices you might have to make later? Could you shorten the vacation or stay closer to home, and put half of that money toward paying off the loan? What if your company matches your 401(k) contribution up to 3 percent of your salary? Are you going to gain more from claiming the matching funds and earning a 4 percent return on the savings you sock away, or from using that money to quickly pay off a private student loan with a 12 percent interest rate?

Some trade-offs, particularly those that promise long-term bene-fits like retirement savings or career advancement, may be worth making, and there may be times when, for personal reasons, you choose instant gratification over paying off your loans earlier. At least you are making a conscious choice and weighing the conse-quences of your actions. When you are aware that you are mak-ing a choice, you are less likely to act irresponsibly or in a way that drives you further into debt.

Know Your Financial Realities

The first step to your future financial security is having a clear understanding of your present circumstances. Based on this un-derstanding you will be able to identify your needs and your re-sources, develop a plan of action, and regularly evaluate your progress to see whether you are still on course.

Income and Outcome

Begin by making a list of all your financial assets, including the money in your checking and savings accounts, investments, and savings bonds. If possible, use a spreadsheet on a computer so that you can do calculations and rearrange the information easily.

Next, write down your regular monthly income from all sources. If your income comes at intervals from commissions, contracts, or royalties, write down what you have received over the last six months, and any payments you expect to receive within the next three months, and divide the total by nine. This should be reliable income that you are certain of receiving; note tentative income and pending contracts separately.

Now, take a look at your bank statement and credit card statements for the last month, and in another column, write down the amount you have withdrawn from each account. Subtract any major one-time expenditures, such as the purchase of an appliance or payment of a large medical bill.

Add up your income and your expenditures, and compare them. If your expenditures for the last month were greater than your income, you need to act quickly to avoid going deeper into debt. Think about how last month compares to other months of the year; was it a typical month, or a month in which you had extra expenses, such as property taxes or Christmas shopping? Are there months when you spend less to compensate?

Now make a list of everything you owe: student loans, credit card balances, mortgage, and money you borrowed from a friend or parent.

Create a "Picture" of Your Student Loans

Gather all your student loan documents together and create a chart or a spreadsheet of all your loans. You can begin by going online and looking up your federal loans in the National Student

Loan Data System, at **www.nslds.ed.gov**. Details of private and federal loans obtained through Sallie Mae can be found at **SallieMae.com**. If you borrowed directly from a private lender, look up the information on your promissory note and loan documents, or contact the loan servicer directly.

On a chart or spreadsheet, write down the name and contact information of the loan servicer for each loan, including a telephone number and Web URL, and your account number. Beside each loan, write down the type of loan, the school you attended, the date when the loan was disbursed, the amount of the loan principal, the interest rate, the amount of principal and interest outstanding, the term of the loan, the repayment plan, and the monthly payment and due date. If you have a consolidation loan, remember that it was used to pay off underlying loans that are no longer outstanding. **FinAid.org** has a convenient chart, at **www.finaid.org/loans/studentloanchecklist.phtml**, that you can print and fill in. This loan "picture" will help you understand your obligations and make decisions about paying off or consolidating loans. It will also serve as a reference when you need to contact your loan servicer.

It is impossible to say exactly how much you will finally pay; the amount is affected by the length of time over which you pay the loan off, whether you have periods of forbearance or make extra payments, and variations in interest rates. You can use calculators, however, to estimate how much you will pay under different circumstances. Add a column to your loan chart showing how much you will pay if the loan is paid off in ten years. Update the chart whenever you make extra payments to bring down the loan balance.

Loan "Picture" for Student Graduating in 2007 and Entering Repayment 11/5/2007

School & Type of Loan	Loan Servicer	Origination & End Date	Amt of Loan	Principal Outstanding 9/22/2008	Interest Outstanding 1/31/2009	Interest	Interest Rate	Status	Monthly Payment Amount	Repaymt 10 Years
Direct Loan - UF	DIRECT LOAN SERVICING CENTER, PO Box 5609, Greenville, TX 75403-5609 https://www.dl.ed.gov/borrower	8/25/2003 4/30/2004	$623	$382	$5	Variable	4.21%	Repayment Standard Repayment Plan	$50 on 28th of every month	
Direct Loan - UF	DIRECT LOAN SERVICING CENTER, PO Box 5609, Greenville, TX 7540-35609	8/23/2004 8/5/2005	$2,625	$1,555	$23	Variable	4.21%	Repayment Standard Repayment Plan		
Direct Loan - UF	DIRECT LOAN SERVICING CENTER, PO Box 5609, Greenville, TX 75403-5609	8/22/2005 5/5/2006	$1,195	$733	$11	Variable	4.21%	Repayment Standard Repayment Plan		$3,010
Direct Loan - UF	DIRECT LOAN SERVICING CENTER, PO Box 5609, Greenville, TX 7540-35609	8/28/2006 5/4/2007	$1,868	$1,142	$27	Fixed	6%	Repayment Standard Repayment Plan		$1,246
Private Loan - Signature	SALLIE MAE 888-272-5543 www.salliemae.com	10/24/2006	$16,139	$15,450	$688.88	Variable	6.25%	Repayment Standard Repayment Plan	$164 on the 24th of every month	$21,745
Total				$19,262	$755				$214	$26,001

Your Credit Report Card

What is a Credit Score?

Every time you apply for a new bank account or credit card, a business loan, an automobile loan, or a mortgage, your lender looks at your credit history to evaluate the risk involved in loaning you money. Your credit report is in an indication of your willingness and your ability to repay the loan, and it is as important as your diploma in predicting your financial future. Your credit report determines whether your loan application will be accepted, the amount of credit you will be given, and the interest rate you will pay. It may also determine how much you pay for automobile and homeowners insurance. Employers, landlords, and insurance companies also look at your credit report for evidence that you are responsible and reliable. An adverse credit report could cost you a job for which you are otherwise a perfect candidate.

Three nationwide credit reporting agencies, Experian (**www.experian.com**), TransUnion (**www.transunion.com**), and Equifax (**www.equifax.com/home**), gather financial data and compile reports on individual consumers. Each agency uses different methodologies and is constantly trying to increase the accuracy of its reports, so the information on each report is a little different. Ironically, if you act responsibly, pay for everything in cash, and never borrow money, you may be turned down when you do apply for a loan because you have little or no credit history. Credit reports include information on credit card accounts; retail store and gas station cards; bank loans; auto loans and leases; mortgages and home equity lines of credit; credit union loans; consumer finance accounts; and student loans. They tend not to include information on checking accounts or smaller credit accounts, or payment history for rent, utility bills, or medical bills, unless they have become delinquent and been sent to collection.

Credit reports also include information from public records, such as court judgments, tax liens, bankruptcy filings, and collection accounts. This type of adverse information can cause problems because it is not always updated when the problem has been resolved, the debt has been paid off, or the ruling has been challenged by the consumer on the grounds that it is inaccurate. Credit reports also record the companies that have requested your credit information over the past two years.

Increasingly, creditors, insurance companies, employers, and landlords look at your credit score instead of — or together with — your credit history. A credit score is a number derived from your credit history information and is considered an indicator of how credit-worthy you are. The original model for calculating a credit score was developed by the Fair Isaac Corporation, whose FICO credit score has become the industry standard. Each of the credit reporting agencies has developed its own unique formulas using the Fair Isaac model to assign credit scores. The FICO score is derived by combining historical information about an individual with statistical data, and the various components of the score are weighted according to their importance. You can see the components that make up a FICO score, and the current interest rates charged for auto loans and mortgages according to FICO score, at **www.myFICO.com**. FICO scores range from 620 to 850, and a score over 760 is considered very good.

Savvy Student Tip:

Credit scores are used to determine interest rates for private student loans. Though a young college student is not likely to have a well-established credit history, lenders use credit scores to help determine the interest rate for private student loans. Having a cosigner with a high credit score can significantly reduce the interest rate on a private loan. FICO recommends checking your FICO score six months before you anticipate needing a student loan, to give yourself time to raise your score and correct any errors.

Student Loans and Credit Reports

In May 2008, Sallie Mae erroneously reported loans that were in graduated repayment as partial payments to the credit bureaus. Overnight, the Equifax credit scores of over a million borrowers dropped more than 100 points. The error was quickly corrected, but it demonstrated the powerful effect of student loan delinquencies on credit scores.

A student loan in good standing does not have an adverse effect on your credit report or credit score. A student loan in deferment or forbearance is considered to be a loan in good standing. Delinquent student loan payments or loans in default have a negative effect on your credit score and may prevent you from getting a mortgage, car payment, or apartment rental. A student loan default remains on your credit report for seven years. As soon as you rehabilitate a defaulted student loan, the default will be removed from your credit report, and your loan will be reported as a loan in good standing.

Lenders regularly report on-time loan payments, as well as delinquent payments and defaults, to the credit bureaus. A history of steady, on-time student loan payments over several years helps establish a strong credit history and contributes to a higher credit score.

Establishing Your Credit History

A positive credit history and good credit score are not established overnight. More than 50 million Americans — including immigrants, teenagers, and people who have always applied for credit in a spouse's name — have little or no credit history.

- The first step is to get on the credit "radar" by applying for some kind of credit, such as a secured or low-balance credit card, and using it sparingly. Many credit card companies recruit college students by going to campuses and offering free gifts such as T-shirts to students who apply for their credit cards. These credit card offers are dangerous; a single late payment can send the interest rate skyrocketing, and the credit limit soon increases from a few hundred dollars to two or three thousand, tempting a student further into debt. If you can use one of these credit cards responsibly, making an occasional purchase and paying it off by the due date, you will gradually establish your credit history. You will know you are on your way when you start to receive more favorable credit card offers from other companies.

- Do not open more than one or two new accounts per year, because too many new accounts have a negative impact on your credit rating.

- Use less than 50 percent of the available credit on each account. The ratio of outstanding credit balances to available credit is another component of your credit score.

- Do not "shop around" too much for consumer credit. An excessive number of credit applications brings down your credit score. If you are looking for new private student loans, submit your applications and do price comparisons within a 30-day period rather than over an extended period of time.

- Pay all your bills on time, including cell phone, medical bills, utilities, electricity, rent, and parking tickets. Even a minor late payment, if reported, can lower your credit score. There is a growing movement to establish alternative credit scores, such as the FICO Expansion score, for consumers who have no prior credit relationships. FICO partners with Pay Rent, Build Credit, Inc. (PRBC), at **www.prbc.com**, and enables consumers and small business owners to build a credit rating based on their history of making rent and other recurring bill payments. PRBC charges a fee to verify payment information entered by individuals. PRBC reports and FICO Expansion scores are accepted by some lenders, insurers, and employers as proof of creditworthiness. First American Credco, LexisNexis, and TransUnion also gather information about individuals' payment histories for lenders.

- Check your credit report regularly. Section 211 of the Fair and Accurate Credit Transactions Act of 2003 provides for every consumer to receive one free credit report annually from each of the three major consumer credit reporting agencies (Experian, TransUnion, and Equifax). This can be ordered online from AnnualCreditReport.com (**www.annualcreditreport.com/cra/index.jsp**), created by the three credit bureaus to fulfill this requirement. You can also obtain your free credit report by calling 1-877-322-8228 or by mailing a request form (**www.annualcreditreport.com/cra/requestformfinal.pdf**) to:

Annual Credit Report Request Service
P.O. Box 105281
Atlanta, GA 30348-5281

Savvy Student Tip:

*Do not be taken in by offers of "free credit reports." A number of online businesses offer a "free credit report" as a means of recruiting customers for fee-based credit protection services. **AnnualCreditReport. com** is the only official site where you can obtain your annual credit report without any fee or further obligation*

A+
SAVVY
STUDENT

Under federal law, you are also entitled to a credit report within 60 days of receiving notice that a company has taken negative action against you, such as denying your application for credit, insurance, or employment. The notice should contain the name, address, and phone number of the consumer reporting company that provided the financial information. You are also entitled to one free report a year if you are receiving welfare, are unemployed and plan to look for a job within 60 days, or if your report is inaccurate because of fraud, including identity theft. Otherwise, a consumer reporting bureau may charge up to $10.50 for an additional copy of your report, if requested within a 12-month period.

You can request the free reports from each of the credit reporting agencies at different times during the year, giving you an opportunity to see whether your credit report has improved or deteriorated because of any actions you have taken. Each agency's report is slightly different, but the key information will be similar.

Resolving Problems with Your Credit Report

If you find errors or incomplete information in your credit report, including misspelled names, old addresses, or an incorrect report from an information provider, contact the consumer credit agency and the information provider. Unfamiliar accounts or creditors on your report may indicate fraud or identity theft, or simply a mix-up of some kind. Query any unfamiliar information to discover its source; often a creditor does business under another name that you might not know about.

Under federal law, both the consumer reporting company and the information provider — that is, the person, company, or organization that provides information about you to a consumer reporting company — are responsible for correcting inaccurate or incomplete information in your credit report. Send the details of the error in writing to the consumer credit agency. It must investigate within 30 days and notify the information provider of the inaccuracies, and the information provider must review the information and report the results of its investigation to the consumer credit bureau. If the disputed information is found to be inaccurate, the information provider must report this to all three credit bureaus. The consumer credit agency must provide you with a written account of the results, and another free credit report if a change has been made.

Also send a written notice to the creditor or information provider that you are disputing an inaccuracy in information reported to a consumer credit agency. If the information provider reports the item to a credit agency it must include a notice of your dispute, and if the item is found to be incorrect, the provider may not report it to a credit agency again. If your dispute with the consumer reporting agency is not resolved, you can request that a record of it be included in your credit file and in future credit reports. You can also request that a copy be sent to anyone who recently requested your credit report. The consumer agency will charge a fee for this.

Savvy Student Tip:

You do not need to subscribe to a "credit monitoring" service. Unless you are already a victim of identity theft or fraud, you do not need to subscribe to one of the paid "credit monitoring" services marketed by many financial companies. You can monitor your own credit by checking your credit reports once a year, keeping an eye on bank and credit card statements, and following up if you are turned down for a loan application.

CHAPTER 10

Choosing a
Student Loan
Repayment Plan

Federal education loans offer four main repayment plans. The repayment options for a private loan are defined in the loan contract and vary from lender to lender. The type of payment plan that is best for you depends on your financial circumstances when you graduate and your plans for the future. You have the option of prepaying your federal student loans at any time without penalty if you suddenly come into a substantial amount of cash. Private lenders may impose a penalty for early repayment, depending on the loan contract.

You may switch from one plan to another by contacting your lender. FFEL lenders must allow you to switch at least once each year, but most will allow you to switch more often if your financial circumstances make it necessary. Borrowers with Direct Loans may change plans at any time by notifying the Department of Education. If you are repaying your Direct Loan through an income-contingent or income-based repayment plan, you cannot change plans until you have made payments in each of the previous three months before requesting the change. You cannot switch from an extended or graduated payment plan to an income-contingent plan if the loan has been in repayment for more than 25 years.

Savvy Student Tip:

Whenever possible, pay more than your scheduled monthly payment. Notify your loan processor that you want the excess payment applied to the principal of the loan, since reducing the principal will reduce the amount of interest you pay over the life of the loan. Lenders are allowed to credit any payment received first to accrued late charges or collection costs, then to any outstanding interest, and finally to outstanding principal. This is also true for schools collecting Perkins loans and for private loans. If you fail to notify the loan processor that an excess payment is to be applied to the loan principal, it will simply be applied toward your next monthly payment..

Standard Repayment Plan

Under a standard repayment plan, you make a fixed monthly payment for a term of up to ten years. If your loan was not a large one, the term may be shorter, but most college graduates need at least ten years to pay off their loans. There is a $50 minimum monthly payment. For graduates who find a well-paid job soon after leaving college, this is the best option. Standard payment plans offer the best interest rate of all the repayment plans.

Extended Repayment Plan

Under an extended repayment plan, fixed loan payments are stretched out over a longer term of 12 to 30 years, depending on the amount of the loan. The size of each payment is reduced, but the additional interest you will pay over the extended term will increase the total amount repaid over the lifetime of the loan. The smaller monthly payments are easier to manage when your income is low, you have many monthly bills and obligations, or you have had financial setbacks. The minimum monthly payment is $50.

Extended repayment is not available for FFEL loan balances disbursed before October 7, 1998, or for balances less than $30,000.

If you choose this option, do not just set up automatic debit and forget about it. Make larger payments whenever you can afford to. If your financial circumstances improve dramatically, increase the amount you pay regularly every month as much as you can.

Graduated Repayment Plan

A graduated repayment plan starts out with lower payments, which gradually increase every two years. The loan term is 12 to 30 years, depending on the total amount borrowed. The monthly payment must at least cover the interest that accrues, and must also be a minimum of $25. The monthly payment can be no less than 50 percent and no more than 150 percent of the monthly payment under the standard repayment plan. A graduated repayment plan is appropriate when you start your career with a modest income that you expect will rise steadily over time. It will pay off your loan faster than an extended repayment plan, but allow you some flexibility when you are starting your career.

Income-Contingent Repayment Plan

The Income Contingent Repayment (ICR) plan is designed to make repaying education loans easier for students who intend to pursue jobs with lower salaries, such as careers in public service. The amount of the monthly payments is based on the borrower's income, family size, and total amount borrowed. The monthly payment amount is adjusted annually, based on changes in annual income and family size, and can be as low as $5 per month.

Income-contingent repayment is currently offered only by the U.S. Department of Education through the Direct Loan program, not to government-guaranteed loans made by banks or other private institutions through the FFEL Program. The maximum repayment period is 25 years. Any debt remaining after 25 years will be discharged (forgiven). Parent loans, such as the Parent PLUS loan, are not eligible.

The federal government's income-contingent repayment formula calculates your monthly payment as the lower of either 20 percent of your monthly discretionary income, defined as your adjusted gross income (AGI) minus the federal poverty line for your family size and state of residence or the amount of the monthly payment under a 12-year standard repayment plan, multiplied by an income percentage factor (IPF) derived from your income and marital status. The latter starts at about 50 percent for incomes near the poverty line. The amount of your monthly payment will be adjusted once a year, depending on your income for the previous year. You will be required to provide qualifying documentation, including proof of income, every year.

An income-contingent repayment plan is appropriate if you have seasonal or wildly-fluctuating income, or work on commission.

It is also a good choice if you start out earning a low income while completing an internship or training, but expect to earn a higher income or have improved financial circumstances later. An average student loan will be almost paid off in 25 years, but if you borrowed $100,000 to go to medical school and then chose a low-paying public service job, the loan forgiveness after 25 years could be a significant benefit.

You can switch to an income-contingent plan at any time, as long as you have not been in repayment for longer than 25 years. If you have at least one Direct Loan, the Department of Education will allow you to consolidate your other FFEL loans into a federal direct consolidation loan in order to qualify for income-contingent repayment. Under certain circumstances, you may qualify to consolidate FFEL loans into a federal direct consolidation loan even if you do not have a Direct Loan. You can pay off your loan or switch to another payment plan whenever you wish.

The benefit of an ICR repayment plan is that your monthly student loan payments will always be affordable. The disadvantage is that if you have a particularly profitable year, the size of your payments will go up accordingly, and you will be obliged to put more of your money into loan payments instead of having it available for other purposes.

The interest rate for an ICR repayment plan is fixed for the lifetime of the loan. The weighted average of the interest rates of the loans included in the program is rounded up to the nearest 1/8th of a percentage point. Students who elect this plan just before their loans enter repayment will be able to lock in the in-school interest rate, which is 3/5th of a percentage point lower.

Savvy Student Tip:

The Income-Sensitive Repayment (ICR program) indirectly subsidizes the interest on a loan with an interest capitalization cap. When the monthly payments are not high enough to cover the interest on your loan, unpaid interest is capitalized (added to the principal) at the end of each year. This capitalization is capped at 10 percent of the original loan amount; any additional unpaid interest continues to accumulate but is not added to the loan balance. As long as you remain in the ICR program, the unpaid interest that is capitalized will not exceed 10 percent of the loan balance and will not be compounded. If you switch to a different repayment plan, all of this accumulated unpaid interest will be added to the loan balance and will begin to be compounded.

The amount of debt discharged after 25 years is treated as taxable income under current law, so be prepared to pay extra taxes the year your loan is discharged. One flaw with the ICR formula for calculating the monthly payment is that it combines the income of married borrowers with that of their spouses, leading to a higher payment amount than the borrower would pay based on his or her own income. The qualifying documents require the spouse's Social Security Number and may require the spouse's signature, essentially making both spouses responsible for the loan. A federal student loan is discharged when the borrower dies, but if the loan is treated as a community property debt, the spouse might still be held responsible. Verify the terms of the loan agreement before signing.

The long repayment term of 25 years makes comparing the relative cost of an extended repayment plan with the cost of the ICR plan complicated. Using the ICR plan, you will repay slightly more over the lifetime of the loan than you would under the 25-

year extended repayment plan, but if you account for inflation, the actual value of your payments can be significantly less. The value of a dollar will decrease over time, and the average salary will increase. With the ICR plan, you will be making larger payments later on when the dollar has less buying power than it does now. You can use the Income Contingent Repayment Calculator on Finaid.org (**www.finaid.org/calculators/icr.phtml**) to compare the ICR program with standard and extended repayment plans, by entering various scenarios such as a change in salary or an increase in the size of your family. The FinAid ICR calculator computes the net present value (NPV) of the total payments, and gives you their value in constant dollars. Using constant dollars to compare student loans provides a more realistic picture of the difference in actual value. Using constant dollars, the cost of a 25-year extended repayment plan is substantially greater than the cost of an ICR plan.

Income-Sensitive Repayment Plan (ISR)

Income-sensitive repayment (ISR) is similar to income-contingent repayment (ICR) but is for loans serviced by lenders in the FFEL program. It makes monthly loan payments easier for borrowers with temporarily low incomes. The borrower can choose a fixed percentage of his or her gross monthly income, between 4 and 25 percent, as the amount of the monthly loan payment. Some lenders use your debt-to-income ratio to calculate a minimum percentage of your income that must be applied to your loan every month.

The monthly payment must at least cover the interest on the loan, which is equal to the loan principal multiplied by the interest rate and divided by 12. You must reapply for income-sensitive repayment each year and provide income documentation, including income tax returns and/or W-2 statements. Income-sensitive repayment is limited to a ten year repayment term. It may temporarily decrease the monthly payment amount compared with a standard repayment plan, but the size of the monthly payments will increase when your income increases. With an income-sensitive repayment plan, you may pay more interest over the lifetime of your loan than with a standard repayment plan. If you think you will need income-sensitive repayment for longer than one year, extended or graduated repayment plans that reduce the size of your monthly payments by increasing the term of your loan might be a better choice.

Income-Based Repayment (IBR)

The Income-Based Repayment (IBR) plan is part of the College Cost Reduction and Access Act of 2007 and became available on July 1, 2009. Income-based repayment is only available for federal student loans, such as the Stafford, Grad PLUS, and consolidation loans. It is not available for Parent PLUS loans or for consolidation loans that include Parent PLUS loans. Perkins loans are eligible if they are part of a consolidation with other qualified loans.

IBR is an alternative to ISR and ICR plans, which will both continue to be available. It is intended to encourage students to pursue jobs with lower salaries, such as careers in public service. Monthly loan payments are capped at 15 percent of your monthly discretionary income, which is calculated as the difference between your adjusted gross income (AGI) and 150 percent of the federal poverty line for your family size and the state in which you reside. There is no minimum monthly payment. After 25 years of repayment, any remaining debt will be discharged (forgiven). You must initially sign up for 25-year income-based repayment, but you can pay off your loan or switch to another repayment plan at any time. Borrowers who consolidate into Direct Lending in order to obtain public service loan forgiveness are limited to the IBR, ICR, and standard repayment plans.

A new public service loan forgiveness program will discharge the remaining debt after ten years of full-time employment in public service. The borrower must have made 120 payments on the Direct Loans for which forgiveness is requested in order to obtain this benefit. Only payments made on or after October 1, 2007 count toward the required 120 monthly payments. The years of employment in public service do not have to be continuous, and education awards for service programs such as the Peace Corps and AmeriCorps are counted as part of the 120 payments. Borrowers may consolidate other loans into the Direct Lending program in order to qualify.

If monthly payments under the IBR program are not large enough to cover the accrued interest on a subsidized Stafford loan, the federal government will also waive or subsidize the unpaid interest for the first three years.

The IBR program is appropriate for students who will be pursuing public service careers and borrowers with a large debt and low income, or a large household .If your financial difficulties are only temporary, an economic hardship deferment may be a better option.

The IBR plan will typically result in the lowest monthly payment for many low-income borrowers and is an alternative to going into default. An IBR repayment calculator on Finaid.org (**www.finaid.org/calculators/ibr.phtml**) lets you compare the outcome of different loan repayment plans in constant dollars.

Under the original IBR legislation, the combined income and student loan debt of married couples was used to calculate the cap on monthly payments. An amendment passed by Congress in December 2007 allows a married borrower to file his or her income tax as "married filing separately" and count only his or her adjusted gross income (AGI) and student loan debt in the calculation (P.L. 110-153, December 21, 2007).

Income-based repayment is probably preferable to income-contingent repayment, particularly if the borrower's financial circumstances improve, because it caps the monthly payment at a lower percentage of discretionary income and defines "discretionary income" as a smaller portion of the borrower's gross income (AGI). If a borrower is employed in public service, the loan forgiveness after ten years of payments is a significant benefit. Under current law, the amount of debt discharged is treated as taxable income in the year the loan is forgiven, so be prepared.

Repayment Options for Private Loans

Private lenders are not required to offer the same repayment options as federal loans. Repayment options vary from lender to lender. Most lenders offer some form of extended payment plans, deferment, and forbearance, but the requirements may be different or they may charge additional fees. Review your private loan contracts carefully to understand what rights you have. If you are in danger of default because of financial difficulties, some lenders may offer options that are not specifically spelled out in the loan contract; you will not know about them until you ask.

Most lenders will allow for repayment terms of 15, 20, or even 25 years, subject to a required minimum payment of $25 or $50 per month. Many lenders provide repayment calculators on their Web sites that compare payment amounts using different repayment periods. These calculators give a general idea what the payments will be, but the actual payment amount will depend on the "risk-based price" — that is, the interest rate based on the individual borrower's credit risk — that was determined when the loan was approved.

What Plan is Best for You?

You will pay the least for your loans, and become free of debt most quickly, if you opt for the Standard Repayment Plan and pay off the entire loan in ten years or less. Your financial realities, though, may make it necessary to choose a different repayment plan. Most financial advisors recommend that your student loan payment be between 10 and 15 percent of your annual gross income (AGI). Any more than that and you are likely to encounter financial hardships and have difficulty making your payments. Taking on responsibility for children or other dependents will increase your monthly expenses, so you will need to increase your monthly income in order to maintain the same loan payments.

In calculating the payments for income-based repayment plans, and documenting eligibility for economic hardship deferment, the

Federal Government and the Department of Education use a formula based on household size and the annual poverty guidelines established by the Department of Health and Human Services to define discretionary income. Student loan payments exceeding a certain percentage of that discretionary income constitute "partial economic hardship." If your monthly loan payment under a Standard Repayment Plan exceeds 15 percent of your annual gross income, you should consider changing to a payment plan that allows you to make lower monthly payments, at least until your financial circumstances improve. You can still make additional loan payments whenever you have some extra cash.

Your plans for the future also affect your choice of repayment plan. If you anticipate a career in which your income will always be low, an income-contingent or income-based plan will keep your payments affordable, and any balance still outstanding after 25 years will be forgiven. Graduates going into public service careers should also choose income-contingent or income-based plans. Income-contingent plans are also appropriate if your ability to earn an income is limited by the onset of a partial disability, or by responsibility for the care of a disabled child or elderly family member.

Student loan repayment calculators on Finaid.org (**www.finaid. org/calculators/scripts/loanpayments.cgi**) and CollegeBoard. com (**http://apps.collegeboard.com/fincalc/sla.jsp**) help to estimate what your monthly loan payment will be under a Standard Repayment Plan. You can visit sites like Careersnet.com (**www. careersnet.com/salary.html**) or NYJobsource.com (**http://nyjob-source.com/salary.html**) to find the expected average salary for specific careers.

Sample Salaries and Affordable Loan Payments

Career	Mean Annual Salary*	Affordable Monthly Student Loan Payment
Accountants and Auditors	$58020.00	$483.50
Architects	$68560.00	$571.33
Chemists	$63470.00	$528.92
Dentists	$131210.00	$1093.42
Economists	$80900.00	$674.17
Engineering Teachers, College	$78780.00	$656.50
Family and General Practitioners	$139640.00	$1163.67
Food Service Managers	$42010.00	$350.08
Human Resource Officers	$48470.00	$403.92
Legislators	$31490.00	$262.42
Mechanical Engineers	$70000.00	$583.33
Microbiologists	$63360.00	$528.00
Political Science Professors	$65760.00	$548.00
Registered Nurses	$51230.00	$426.92

Salary data from the Bureau of Labor Statistics, 2007

CHAPTER 11

Managing Your Loan Payments

S tudent loans offer a number of features not available with other types of loans, designed to help a borrower avoid default and keep up regular loan payments. Other types of loans are approved based on the borrower's existing credit history. A student borrower is typically too young to have a credit history and will not have a steady income until after all the loan money has been spent. Student loans allow borrowers to adjust their payments to fit their financial circumstances, and even to delay payment during periods of unemployment, volunteer, and military service. Many loans also offer lower interest rates as incentives for borrowers who sign up for electronic debits and make consistent payments.

Eligibility requirements for deferment and student loan forgiveness change frequently. If you are employed in public service, or if you believe you might qualify for some form of debt relief, check the most recent developments regularly on the Department of Education Web site.

Student loan management has three primary objectives:

- Lower the amount you have to pay

- Adjust loan payments to fit your financial circumstances

- Avoid default

Your lender is not silently monitoring the ups and downs of your financial affairs or the changes in your personal circumstances. It is up to you to recognize when you need to make changes, and to ask for financial relief when you need it. There may be a time when you find yourself unable to make regular loan payments, such as during a period of temporary unemployment or military service. You can temporarily delay making payments by requesting deferment or forbearance. Lenders make it easy to apply for deferment and forbearance, but in most situations, you must fill out and submit the application and accompanying documentation.

Lowering Your Interest Rate

As we discussed in the section on interest, a half of one percent may seem like a small number, but when you are calculating interest over a repayment period of ten or twenty years, it can add up to a considerable sum of money. You will want to consider any option that will lower your interest rate because it means big savings in the long run. Many lenders offer interest rate reductions — typically 0.25 percent — if you sign up for automatic debits from your checking account or for electronic billing. Lenders also offer interest rate reductions as a reward for making payments on time, for example, a 1-percent reduction after you make the first 24 or 36 consecutive payments on time, for as long as you continue to be on time. You will lose this reduction if a single payment is late, and until now, only 10 percent of borrowers have been able to retain it; electronic banking may make it easier for future borrowers to keep up.

You can also lower your interest rate by consolidating your loans into a single loan with a lower interest rate. We will discuss consolidation shortly. If you have a private student loan with a high interest rate, consider taking out another type of loan to pay it off. After you have been employed for a few years and have a good credit rating, you could use a promotional 0 percent APR offer to move the balance to a credit card and then pay it off. Just read the fine print and allow for balance transfer fees and time limits on the low interest rate. A home equity loan can also serve as a lower-interest alternative, although you may lose student loan features, like the ability to request forbearance and deferment, eligibility to have an employer pay off your student loans, and tax deductions for interest paid on student loans. This solution does not apply to government loans, which have a low interest rate and qualify for numerous loan forgiveness programs if you go into teaching, health care, the military, or public service.

Deferment

Certain conditions qualify you for a loan deferment on federally guaranteed loans, a period during which student loan payments are suspended. The interest on loans in deferment is lower than the interest on loans in repayment or forbearance. Interest on government subsidized loans is paid by the government during deferment periods. The interest that accrues on unsubsidized loans during the deferment period will be added to the loan balance — or capitalized — and increase the total amount that you will repay in the long run, so it is wise to make at least the interest payments if possible. You do not jeopardize your deferment status if you make payments on a loan during a period of deferment.

If you have already defaulted on your loans, you are not eligible for deferment.

If you meet all the eligibility requirements, your lender cannot deny deferment. Your Master Promissory Note must have been signed during the years for which the deferment is allowed. You must complete all the necessary paperwork and submit it to your lender using the most recent version of the application form; because deferment is offered through the federal government, your lender cannot accept outdated or incomplete forms. Deferment forms for Direct Loans are available on the Federal Student Aid Web site, at **www.dl.ed.gov/borrower/DefermentFormList. do?cmd=initializeContext**, and for other federally-guaranteed loans on **www.Salliemae.com**.

In-school Deferments

If you are enrolled in and attending an accredited institution of higher learning at least half-time, you qualify for an in-school deferment on federally-guaranteed loans. Parent PLUS loans do not qualify for deferment unless they predate 1986 or the parents are now students themselves. There is not a time limit on the deferment, as long as you are actively enrolled in school. The deferment may be revoked if you stop attending classes. If you take a semester off or transfer to another school, it is your responsibility to inform your lender.

Graduate Fellowship Deferments

This deferment applies to students pursuing graduate studies outside the classroom, such as research, teaching, or independent study. In order to qualify, you must hold a bachelor's degree, have been recommended to the program, and have your status certified by an official of the program. The graduate fellowship deferment is available on Stafford, Perkins, and Direct loans, for parent borrowers of PLUS loans taken out before 1993.

Rehabilitation Training Programs

Deferments are available for borrowers participating in programs designed to overcome mental or physical disabilities, or drug or alcohol addiction. The rehabilitation program must be approved by a state or federal regulatory agency and by the Department of Education. The program must offer individualized services to assist the borrower in overcoming the limitations of his or her condition and must have an expected date of completion. The borrower must be unable to work or attend school full-time as a result of participation in the rehabilitation program. An official of the program must certify that the borrower is participating in the program and give specific starting and ending dates. This deferment applies to borrowers of Stafford and PLUS loans, and to parent borrowers of PLUS loans disbursed prior to 1993.

Unemployment Deferment

An unemployment deferment is available for borrowers who are working less than 30 hours a week (substantially unemployed). You can obtain this deferment by qualifying for state unemployment benefits or registering with an employment agency and actively seeking full-time employment in any field. You do not have to document your job search for the first six-month period of deferment, but in order to obtain an extension, you will need to demonstrate that you have applied for employment with at least six companies during the past six months. You can extend this deferment for up to three years, depending on the age of your loan. Loans issued prior to 1993 are eligible for 24 months of deferment; those issued after 1993 are eligible for 36 months. The unemployment deferment is available for Stafford, Perkins, and Direct loans, and for parent borrowers of PLUS loans if the parent is unemployed.

You do not have to have been previously employed to qualify for the unemployment deferment. If you have not found employment by the time your grace period expires, you should seek an unemployment deferment.

Military Deferment

All federally-insured student loans can be deferred for active or retired members of the military service and National Guard who are called to active duty during a war, other military operation, or national emergency. This deferment may be requested by the borrower or the borrower's representative. The previous three-year time limit on military deferment was eliminated in 2007, and there is no longer any time limit. Eligibility for the deferment ends 180 days after the borrower is demobilized from active duty service.

An Active Duty Student Deferment program began October 1, 2007 for students enrolled more than half-time in an institute of higher education who are called for active duty and plan to return to school after they have completed their service. This defer-ment is available for students called to active duty at the time, or within six months prior to the time, that they were enrolled in school. To qualify, the student borrower must be on active duty, but not necessarily during a war or other military emergency. The deferment period expires either 13 months after completion of active duty military service or when the student re-enrolls in school, whichever occurs first.

Economic Hardship Deferment

The Economic Hardship Deferment provides relief for borrowers who have difficulty meeting their monthly payments but do not qualify for the Unemployment Deferment. It is particularly im-portant for medical students during an internship or residency.

The Economic Hardship Deferment replaces the career-related, new baby, and temporary disability deferments that existed be-tween 1987 and 1993, and is available only on loans issued after July 1993.

You are automatically eligible for the Economic Hardship Defer-ment if you qualified previously for another economic hardship deferment under another federal loan program such as a Perkins loan; are receiving federal or state assistance, such as TANF, SSI, Food Stamps, or state general public assistance; or are serving in the Peace Corps. You are also eligible if your monthly income from full-time employment does not exceed the larger of either the federal minimum wage or 150 percent of the poverty line in-come for your family size and state. The poverty line for a fam-ily of two living in the 48 contiguous states was $14,000 in 2008.

Current documentation such as pay stubs, income tax returns, or copies of assistance award letters will be required. **Finaid.org** has an Economic Hardship calculator, at **www.finaid.org/calculators/economichardship.phtml**, which can determine your eligibility for this deferment.

The Economic Hardship Deferment is available in one-year increments for two or three years, depending on when your loan was initiated.

Loans Issued Between 1987 and 1993

Between 1987 and 1993, the government allowed a number of deferments for medical interns and residents, teachers who worked in an area where teachers were in short supply, parental leave, working mothers of young children, temporary disability, public servants, and the military. These deferments are still available to borrowers whose loans were issued before 1993. Application forms for these deferments can be found under "Forms" at the Federal Student Aid Web site, at **www.dl.ed.gov/borrower**.

Perkins Loan Deferments

Perkins loan deferments are available only to borrowers of Perkins loans. Borrowers who qualify for these deferments are generally eligible for a total or partial discharge of their student loans after they have been employed in public service positions for a specified period of time. Perkins loan deferments include:

- Teacher serving students from low-income families

- Special Education Teacher

- Provider of Early Intervention Services for the Disabled

- Teacher of Math, Sciences, Language, or a Teacher Shortage area

- Public or Non-profit Family Services

- Nurse or Medical Technician

- Law Enforcement or Corrections Officer

- Head Start program

- VISTA or Peace Corps

Military

To apply for a deferment, contact the school that issued the loan or the agency servicing your loan. Interest on Perkins Loans is subsidized by the government during deferment periods.

Forbearance

If you do not qualify for deferments, or hold private student loans, you can request forbearance from your lender. Forbearance is permission to temporarily delay loan payments during a period of financial difficulty. It can also involve granting an extension to your payment period or approving lower payments. You might need to request forbearance if you are ineligible for in-school deferment because you are attending classes less than half-time; if poor health impacts your ability to work or make payments; if you have exceeded the deferment period for unemployment; if your work hours are suddenly reduced; or if you experience a life-changing event, such as the birth of a baby or the death of a spouse.

Most forbearance is granted at the discretion of your lender, and lenders' policies vary widely. Lenders may allow a maximum of from two years (24 months) to five years (60 months) of forbearance. Requirements for qualification depend on the lender's policy guidelines. Some lenders require proof of need for forbearance requests of more than 24 months. Perkins loans allow a maximum of three years and follow income guidelines similar to those of the Economic Hardship Deferment. Many lenders have online forbearance applications. Forbearance agreements may also be made orally over the phone; your lender should send you a written confirmation.

All interest accrued and unpaid during the forbearance period will be capitalized. The federal government does not subsidize interest payments during periods of forbearance as it does with deferments. If possible, you should try to pay at least some of the interest during a forbearance period, because you will face even larger payments when the forbearance is over and the unpaid interest is added to your loan balance. If you are not able to make loan payments because your income is insufficient, consider switching to an income-based payment plan instead.

Forbearance can help you delay going into default if you are already delinquent on your loan payments. Periods of forbearance do not count as part of the nine-month period between your first missed loan payment and the time you enter default

> ## Savvy Student Tip:
>
> *Forbearance is a tool, not a solution. Forbearance should be used as a tool to manage temporary financial difficulties. It should not take the place of a practical plan to make affordable debt payments and stay out of default. While you are in forbearance, the interest on your loan piles up, and that amount is added to your loan balance when the forbearance period ends. If possible, pay at least the interest on your loan while you are in forbearance.*

Discretionary, Mandatory, and Administrative Forbearance

Government FFEL loans make a distinction between discretionary forbearance and mandatory forbearance. Direct Loans do not. Discretionary forbearance allows the lender to determine whether to grant forbearance. Mandatory forbearance on government loans must be granted under certain circumstances, and it is up to the borrower whether to take advantage of it. Deferment programs require the government to appropriate funding for interest payments during the deferment period, but mandatory forbearance can be initiated on short notice and does not cost the government anything. Mandatory forbearance must be granted if:

- You are actively deployed in military service during a war or national emergency

- You are serving in an approved internship or residency program or in a public service program that qualifies for a national educational award

- You qualify for loan forgiveness under certain programs for teachers and the military

- The total amount of your monthly student loan payments is 20 percent or more of your monthly income, in which case you can qualify for an additional three years of forbearance.

Even if you are eligible for mandatory forbearance, you may not want to take it unless you are certain that you will qualify for loan forgiveness under one of the federal programs or will earn a much higher income later on. The interest accrued over several years of forbearance will add substantially to the amount you must ultimately pay off.

Administrative forbearance is automatically imposed by the lender in certain situations, such as while the lender is making a change in the loan's status or a discharge application is being processed. Some lenders may apply administrative forbearance to a delinquent account if the borrower signs up for electronic payment, even when the borrower has already exhausted his or her discretionary forbearance.

Consolidation

What is Loan Consolidation?

Consolidating a loan is something like refinancing a loan. Your lender pays off one or more of your existing student loans and gives you a single new loan with a fixed interest rate. The advantages are that you will have only one loan payment to manage, you may be able to extend your payment period and lower the amount of your monthly payment — though you will end up paying more over the life of the loan if you take longer to pay it off — and you may be able to lock in a lower interest rate. You can also use loan consolidation to become eligible for certain programs, such as the income-contingent repayment plan that is offered only through Direct Loans.

Federal consolidation loans are available through both the Direct Loan and FFEL programs. Almost any type of federal student loan can be consolidated in a Direct consolidation loan, including Subsidized and Unsubsidized Stafford Loans, Supplemental Loans for Students (SLSs), Federally Insured Student Loans (FISLs), PLUS Loans, Direct Loans, Perkins Loans, and Health Education Assistance Loans (HEALs). You must have at least one Direct or FFEL loan to consolidate into a Direct loan. If you have only an FFEL loan, and no Direct loan, you can still consolidate into a Direct Loan if you certify that you were unable to get an FFEL Consolidation Loan or unable to get an FFEL Consolidation Loan with acceptable income-sensitive repayment terms, and that you qualify for the Income-Contingent Repayment Plan.

Savvy Student Tip:

Subsidized Perkins Loans do not retain their interest subsidies during deferment periods if they are consolidated in an FFEL Consolidation Loan. They do retain their subsidies if they are consolidated in Direct consolidation loans.

FFEL lenders are not obligated to accept non-FFEL loans in a consolidation loan. You must have at least one FFEL loan if you want to include non-FFEL loans in a consolidation. Since the economic downturn of 2008, many FFEL lenders have stopped offering consolidation loans, but you can still seek a Direct consolidation loan.

The fixed interest rate on a federal consolidation loan is calculated based on the weighted average of the interest rates of the loans being consolidated, and rounded up to the nearest one-eighth of 1 percent. The interest rate is capped at 8.25 percent. If you consolidate when interest rates have dropped, as they did in 2008, you can lock in low rates for the life of your loan. Federal loans can be consolidated only once. There are a few circumstances in which you will be allowed to consolidate a second time. If you have a federal loan that was not included in your first consolidation, including a new student loan, you can consolidate again. You can also consolidate an FFEL loan into a Direct loan to avoid default by using income-contingent repayment, or to participate in the public service loan forgiveness program.

Private loans cannot be included in a federal consolidation loan. Seek a private consolidation loan only if you want a single monthly payment for your private loans, or if your credit score has improved and you can get a better interest rate for your consolidated loan than you have for your individual loans.

Savvy Student Tip:

Do not consolidate federal loans into a private consolidation loan because you will lose all the rights to deferment, forbearance, affordable repayment, and loan forgiveness offered by government loans.

If you are receiving only one monthly loan bill, it does not mean that your loan has been consolidated. A lender will likely adjust the payments dates of multiple loans so that you will have a single monthly bill and a single due date. Unless you have taken action to consolidate your loans, you still have multiple loans covered by a single Master Promissory Note.

Is Consolidation for You?

If you are still in school, it is probably to your advantage to retain multiple loans. An individual loan may qualify for discharge if a school closes. You may decide to leave school for a semester or continue your education at another school. When you consolidate your loans, you may lose grace periods, loan forgiveness, deferment, forbearance, and other privileges associated with particular loans. A loan consolidation is permanent and cannot be reversed.

Consolidation lessens the payment amount by extending the repayment period farther into the future. If your loan balance is low or you are close to repaying your loans, you may not benefit much from a consolidation.

Interest rates on federal student loans made after July 1, 2006 are fixed, mostly at 6.8 percent. If you have newer loans issued after July 2006, the interest rate for a consolidated loan will also be close to 6.8 percent, and the benefit will be minimal. If you have older loans, on the other hand, you can get a substantial reduction in the interest rate by consolidating when interest rates are much lower than they were when you took out the loans.

Interest rates on federal student loans are .06 percent lower while the borrower has an in-school or other deferment, and during the grace period. If you consolidate during your grace period, you can lock in this reduction for the entire repayment period of the loan.

The Federal Student Aid Web site has a calculator, available at **www.loanconsolidation.ed.gov/loancalc/servlet/common.mvc.**

Controller?controller_task=startCalculator, that you can use to estimate your weighted average interest rate and to see what your loan payments might be under each of the four repayment plans.

Savvy Student Tip:

Since you can only consolidate your loans once, the timing of your consolidation is important. If interest rates on your variable interest loans are high, you will lock in a higher fixed interest rate for the life of your loan. Wait to consolidate when interest rates are lower.

Adjusting Your Payment

According to Sallie Mae, financial experts recommend that your student loan payment should be no more than 10 percent of your monthly income before taxes. When a loan payment consumes too much of your monthly income, it can seriously impact other important financial priorities, such as saving for a down payment on a house, setting aside savings to cover emergencies, buying adequate insurance, and investing for retirement early in your career. An excessive loan payment can even make it impossible for you to pay your monthly bills and can drive you into credit card debt. If your scheduled monthly loan payment is too high to be sustainable on your current income, lower your payment by switching to another payment plan.

Lenders often use your debt-to-income ratio — the percentage of your monthly income that is spent on paying off debt — to determine whether you are capable of taking on additional debt. To calculate your debt-to-income ratio, add up all your monthly debt payments, including your student loans, credit card payments, car payments, and rent, and divide them by your total monthly income. A debt-to-income ratio of 10 percent or less is considered excellent. If your debt-to-income ratio exceeds 21 percent, your resources are overextended. If the ratio is 36 percent or higher, you are in serious financial danger. When your debt-to-income ratio approaches 20 percent, it is a sign that you should seek to lower your monthly student loan payment.

Choose your payment plan based on your current circumstances. Is your current income inadequate because of a temporary situation, such as an illness or the birth of a child? Are you in a poorly paid internship or residency for two years before going on to a more lucrative job? Perhaps your income will always be inadequate because you have chosen a career as a social worker or a teacher in a low-income area. An extended repayment plan will cost more over the life of the loan, but it will give you smaller monthly payments that fit your budget and allow you to pursue other financial goals at the same time. A graduated repayment plan allows you to pay less now and larger monthly payments in later years, when your income has increased. If you are in a low-paid career, income-based repayment plans limit the size of your payments to keep them affordable. Income-based payments will suddenly increase if you switch to a more lucrative career or if you happen to get extra income from another source.

Because you can change repayment plans once a year, you should revisit your repayment plan regularly, especially if your financial circumstances change because of a new job or a layoff, marriage or divorce, inheritance, or business success. Whatever plan you choose, you can always make extra payments to reduce the loan balance. If you have chosen to make lower payments under an extended payment plan, and your monthly income increases substantially, you may want to make larger loan payments to reduce the total amount that you pay for your student loan over time. Compare what you will pay in interest on your student loan with the amount that you could earn by investing the same money in a retirement account and earning interest.

Savvy Student Tip:

If you are not able to afford your loan payments, do not wait until you are delinquent, in default, or over your head in some other kind of debt. Act right away to change your payment plan and lower the amount of your monthly payment.

Going Back to School

Going back to school can be a positive loan management strategy because you can postpone payments using in-school deferment while you earn a professional or graduate degree that may qualify you for a more lucrative career after you leave school. Six months after you leave school or drop to less than half-time enrollment — nine months for Perkins Loans — you must begin repaying your student loans. If you decide to return to school, either to complete your undergraduate degree or as a graduate student, you can request an in-school deferment on those loans and on any new loans you take out. To qualify for in-school deferment, you must be enrolled in an eligible school more than half time and submit a request to your lender. The school you are planning to attend will need to certify your enrollment. A special deferment is available for graduates carrying out their studies outside of the classroom.

Taking out new student loans also provides you with a second opportunity to consolidate at a lower interest rate. Interest will accrue on your unsubsidized loans and be capitalized when you leave school, so pay the interest while you are in school if you can. You cannot receive financial aid or federally guaranteed loans if you have student loans in default or delinquency. Private lenders will not approve a loan for a borrower with bad credit. You will need to rehabilitate or pay off any student loans in delinquency or default before you can receive any financial assistance to pursue further studies.

Contact the financial aid office of your school about financial aid and loan options available to you. In 2008, qualified students seeking a professional or graduate degree were allowed to borrow $20,500 in Stafford Loans per year, with no more than $8,500 of that in subsidized loans. The maximum total debt allowed in Stafford Loans, including undergraduate loans, was $138,500, with no more than $65,500 of that in subsidized loans. For graduate and professional students enrolled in certain approved health profession programs, the total aggregate loan limit was $224,000. Since each school determines its own cost of attendance and expected family contribution (EFC), students are not always given the maximum amount of Stafford Loans.

Graduate and professional degree students can now borrow up to their cost of attendance, minus other estimated financial assistance, through the PLUS Loan Program in both the FFEL and Direct Loan programs. The conditions for graduates applying for PLUS loans are the same as those for parents applying for Parent PLUS loans: the applicant must have an acceptable credit history, and the repayment period begins on the day the loan is disbursed. The interest rate in 2008 was fixed at 8.5 percent for the FFEL program and 7.9 percent for the Direct Loan program. Graduate students must apply for the annual maximum loan under the Subsidized and Unsubsidized Stafford Loan program before they can apply for PLUS loans.

Look for other ways to finance at least part of your graduate or professional degree. Many graduate students work as research or teaching assistants, or get free living accommodations and a small salary for being a resident advisor in undergraduate student housing. You may be able to continue part-time employment. Some employers will contribute to tuition for employees who earn a professional degree in exchange for a work commitment. Numerous federal, state, and private grants and fellowships are available for graduate students in various fields. The Graduate Students section on Students.gov lists numerous funding opportunities (**www.students.gov/STUGOVWebApp/Publi c?topicID=7&operation=topic**).

Savvy Student Tip:

Verify your projected income before accepting a student loan. Some private lenders and professional schools have come under criticism for enticing students to borrow loans for professional degrees by inflating the projected salary for that profession. For example, a high-profile lawyer will earn a much higher salary than an average lawyer working on the staff of a corporation. The higher salary is quoted to prospective borrowers who are assured that they will easily be able to pay off large loans after they graduate. Before you take out additional loans, verify that your expected future income will be sufficient to pay them off. The Bureau of Labor Statistics publishes statistics on average salaries for more than 800 professions, available online at **www.bls.gov/oes/current/oes_nat.htm**.

CHAPTER 12

Getting Someone Else to Pay Off Your Loans

Family and Friends

The people who care the most about your future and your well-being, after yourself, are your family and friends. Ask for help. Let them know that you have graduated, that you are determined to pay off your student loans quickly, and that you would be extremely appreciative of any assistance they would like to give. Tell them that even a small amount will help you reach your goal. If one of your relatives wants to make a substantial payment on your behalf, you can guide them through an online payment or give them the account information so that they can send a check to your lender. That way, they will be confident that the money is going to your student loan repayment and that you are not using it for any other purpose. Be sure to specify to your lender that this payment is to pay down the principal of the loan and is not a regular monthly payment, and specify which loan you want the payment applied to. If any of the money goes toward the loan interest, you may be eligible for a tax deduction even though someone else paid it on your behalf.

Graduation Gifts

If you are planning to send out graduation announcements to all your relatives, register with an online gift site like **GoGift. com,** and tell your family and friends that you would welcome cash gifts to help pay down your student loans. **GoGift.com** will supply you with tissue inserts to include in your graduation announcements. You can also send out e-mail announcements. Registration is free, as are the first two withdrawals (a fee is charged for subsequent withdrawals). Your family members can find your account by going to the Web site and typing in your name. You can create a similar account on **Paypal.com** and send out e-mail announcements. Be sure to send a thank-you note to everyone who gives you a cash gift.

Savings Realized by Using a Cash Gift to Pay Down Loan Principal

Amount of Gift	Loan Principal After Gift	Interest Paid Over 10 Years	Total Amount Paid Over 10 Years	Additional Savings Realized Over 10 Years	Interest Paid Over 30 Years
$0	$10000	$3809	$13809	$0	$13468
$200	$9800	$3733	$13533	$76	$13200
$500	$9500	$3610	$13110	$199	$12794
$1000	$9000	$3428	$12428	$381	$12121
$2000	$8000	$3047	$11047	$762	$10744
$3000	$7000	$2667	$9667	$1142	$9426

Amount of Gift	Total Amount Paid Over 30 Years	Total Amount Paid Over 30 Years	Additional Savings Realized Over 30 Years
$0	$27277	$27277	$0
$200	$26733	$26733	$344
$500	$25904	$25904	$873
$1000	$24549	$24549	$1728
$2000	$21791	$21791	$3486
$3000	$19093	$19093	$5184

This chart illustrates how a cash gift of $500, applied to the principal of a $10,000 student loan when you leave school, could save you an additional $200 if you pay off the loan within ten years.

Upromise

Upromise (**www.upromise.com**) is a marketing initiative that rewards you with savings for college every time you purchase goods or services from one of its partners. You can get 1 to 3 percent back on thousands of eligible items at 21,000 grocery and drug stores, up to 8 percent back when you dine at one of more than 8,000 partner restaurants, and 1 to 25 percent back from eligible purchases made at more than 600 online retailers when you shop through **Upromise.com**. You receive the savings when you use a registered credit card or debit card for payment, or scan a registered drug store or grocery card at the cash register. Savings of $25 or more can be automatically transferred each quarter from your Upromise account directly to your Sallie Mae student loans. Upromise calculates that you can reduce the balance on a $19,000 Stafford loan by $1,000 in ten years if you accumulate $50 in savings annually. Withdrawals are tax free. While you might not accumulate a large amount of savings on your own, you can multiply your savings by enlisting friends and family members to register their debit cards and credit cards so that their savings go into your account.

Grad Gold

Grad Gold (**www.gradgold.com**) partners with hundreds of businesses to earn cash back on online purchases and apply it to your student loan payments. Multiply your savings by asking family members and friends to sign up on your behalf. Earn cash back on travel, office supplies, books, clothing, auto insurance, and just about anything else sold online.

Enlist in the Armed Forces

The Armed Forces offers a Student Loan Repayment Program (SLRP) as an enlistment incentive. You must request SLRP at the time of enlistment or reenlistment, and have it guaranteed in writing in your enlistment contract. You will be required to decline enrolment in the Montgomery GI Bill, score 50 or higher on the Armed Forces Qualifications Test (AFQT), and enlist in one of the crucial Military Occupational Specialties (MOS). The Army will repay as much as $65,000 in qualified education loans (up to $20,000 for reservists), the Navy as much as $65,000, and the Air Force as much as $10,000. SLRP will repay 15 percent of your outstanding loan balance or $500, whichever is greater, each year. There may be additional annual and cumulative caps on the amount repaid.

SLRP repays only federal education loans, such as the Perkins, Stafford, PLUS, or Consolidation loans, not private alternative loans. Defaulted loans are not eligible. Payments made on the borrower's behalf under the SLRP are treated as taxable income for the borrower. Borrowers who are called to active military duty during a war or other military operation or national emergency may now receive a deferment on all outstanding FFEL, Direct Loan, and Federal Perkins Loan programs while they are on active duty and for an additional 180 days after they are demobilized from that active duty service. A new program under the 2008 Higher Education Act reauthorization law prohibits the accrual of interest on Direct Loans disbursed on or after October 1, 2008 while eligible military service members are serving on active duty during a war, military mobilization, or national emergency. Borrowers with FFEL loans may consolidate into the Direct Loan program to take advantage of this benefit.

Additional options, including extended grace periods and in-school deferments, elimination of the three-year limit on Perkins forbearances, forbearances for up to one year granted based on the borrower's written or oral request or the request of a family member or other reliable source, and waiver of certain collection actions while they are in service, are available to members of the national guard called to active duty, reserve or retired members of the Armed Forces called to active duty, active duty members of the Armed Forces who are reassigned, and certain civilians. The active duty service must be in connection with a war, military operation, or national emergency. Eligible civilians are those who reside or are employed in an area that is declared a disaster area by any federal, state, or local official in connection with a national emergency or who suffered direct economic hardship as a direct result of a war, other military operation, or national emergency.

Private loans may be eligible for deferment or forbearance while you are on active military duty; the terms depend on the contract you signed with the lender. You will need to fill out a separate request form and submit it to your private lender. Interest will continue to accrue on your loan during the deferment period. Though the SLRP payments cannot be applied to private loans, you can at least pay down your government loans while receiving a salary and possibly gaining valuable experience and training.

Savvy Student Tip:

Private loans do not qualify for Student Loan Repayment Program. Because your private loans will not be repaid under SLRP, you will still be responsible for the full amount of your private student loans when you come out of the military.

Become a Teacher

Federal Loan Forgiveness for Teachers

The Stafford Loan Forgiveness Program, which became effective on July 1, 2001, gives eligible borrowers loan forgiveness grants of up to $5,000 after they have been employed for at least five consecutive, complete school years as a full-time teacher in a public or private, nonprofit elementary or secondary school that serves low-income families. Highly-qualified math, science, and special education teachers may qualify for loan forgiveness up to $17,500. To find out whether your school is considered a low-income school, visit **www.tcli.ed.gov/CBSWebApp/tcli/TCLI-PubSchoolSearch.jsp**.

You can have up to 100 percent of your Perkins loan forgiven through Perkins Loan Forgiveness if you are a full-time teacher employed in public or nonprofit elementary or secondary schools in districts that were eligible for ESEA Title I-A funding during the time you were teaching there or a school where the percentage of children from low-income families enrolled in the school exceeds 30 percent of total enrollment; or if you are a full-time special-education teacher (including teachers of infants and toddlers), or a full-time teacher of math, science, foreign languages, bilingual education or other fields determined to have a shortage of teachers by the state educational agency.

The Federal Student Aid Web site contains information on loan cancellation for both Stafford and federal Perkins loans, at **http://studentaid.ed.gov/PORTALSWebApp/students/english/teachercancel.jsp.**

The Public Service Loan Forgiveness, which began in 2007 as a result of the College Cost Reduction and Access Act, entitles borrowers who have made 120 payments as part of the Direct Loan program on or after October 1, 2007 to have the remainder of their federal student loan debt — interest and principal — discharged after ten years of full-time employment in public service. Teachers employed in public education or public early childhood education, public librarians, school librarians, and other school-based services, full-time faculty at tribal colleges, and faculties teaching in high-need areas qualify for this program. These borrowers can use the income-based repayment plan (IBR) to keep their 120 monthly loan payments low. Under a standard repayment plan, there would be little or no balance to forgive at the end of ten years. Borrowers can consolidate other federal loans into Direct Lending in order to qualify for this loan forgiveness program.

State Programs

Numerous scholarships and forgivable loans are available for students who plan to become teachers in a "critical need" area or a subject for which there is a shortage of teachers. A number of states offer student loan forgiveness programs for teachers who have already completed their education, if they fulfill certain requirements. The Colorado Loan Incentive for Teachers (LIFT), funded by CollegeInvest and established by the Colorado Commission on Higher Education, allows teachers in high-demand disciplines to receive up to $2,000 a year toward loan repayment for up to four years. (**www.collegeinvest.org/default.aspx?pageID=63**)

Florida's Critical Teacher Shortage Student Loan Forgiveness Program awards eligible Florida teachers up to $2,500 per year to repay undergraduate loans and up to $5,000 per year to repay graduate loans received prior to becoming a certified teacher in a critical teacher shortage subject area. The Mississippi Teacher Loan Repayment Program (MTLR) offers up to $3000 annually for a maximum of four years to assist teachers in paying back their undergraduate loans if they currently hold an Alternate Route Teaching License and currently teach in a Mississippi Teacher Critical Shortage Area or Critical Subject Area (**www.mississippi.edu/riseupms/financialaid-step3-grants-loans.php?article_id=239**). The Oregon Teacher Loan Forgiveness Program forgives federal loans up to $5,000 for teachers who have been employed for five years in a low-income school (**www.getcollegefunds.org/ad_childcare_forgiveness.html**). You can find information on state loan forgiveness programs on the Web site of the American Federation of Teachers, at **www.aft.org/tools4teachers/loan-forgiveness.htm**.

Health Care

Under the Higher Education Opportunity Act of 2008 loan for-giveness program, "full-time professionals engaged in health care practitioner occupations and health care support occupations" and "medical specialists" can qualify for up to $10,000 in student loan forgiveness over five years. Medical specialists are defined as residents participating in a graduate medical education training program or fellowship that has been accredited by the Accredita-tion Council for Graduate Medical Schools (ACGME), requires more than five years of total graduate medical training, and has fewer U.S. medical school graduate applicants nationwide than the total number of positions available under these programs or fellowships. Participants in the loan forgiveness program for ser-vice in areas of national need cannot receive additional repay-ments for the same service under the new public service loan for-giveness program.

Nursing Education Loan Repayment Program

The Nursing Education Loan Repayment Program (NELRP) is a competitive program that repays 60 percent of the qualifying nursing educational loan balance of Registered Nurses (RNs) se-lected for funding in exchange for two years of service at a critical shortage facility. Participants may be eligible to work a third year and receive an additional 25 percent of the qualifying nursing educational loan balance. The American Recovery and Reinvest-ment Act ("Recovery Act") of 2009 provides substantial addition-al funding for the NELRP.

According to the Health Resources and Services Administration of the U.S. Department of Health and Human Services (**http://**

bhpr.hrsa.gov/nursing/loanrepay.htm), a borrower is eligible for loan repayment if he or she:

- Has received a baccalaureate or associate degree in nursing (or an equivalent degree), a diploma in nursing, or a graduate degree in nursing from an accredited school of nursing in a state

- Has outstanding qualifying educational loans obtained for qualifying nursing education leading to a degree or diploma in nursing, as specified above

- Has completed the nursing education program for which the loan balance applies

- Is a U.S. citizen, U.S. national, or a lawful permanent resident of the U.S.

- Is employed full-time (32 hours or more per week) at a critical shortage facility

- Has a current permanent unrestricted license as an RN in the state in which he/she intends to practice or is authorized to practice in that state pursuant to the Nurse Licensure Compact

A borrower is disqualified if he or she has ever defaulted on Federal student loans and certain other debt obligations, even if the borrower has rehabilitated the loan and is now in good standing. Borrowers must submit an application and all required documentation by an annual deadline in order to take advantage of this opportunity.

National Health Service Corps (NHSC)

The National Health Service Corps offers loan forgiveness to physicians and registered nurses who agree to practice for a set number of years in areas that lack adequate medical care, including remote or economically depressed regions.

National Institutes of Health

The U.S. National Institutes of Health's (NIH) Loan Repayment Program repays up to $35,000 per year of student loan debt for US citizens who are conducting clinical medical research. The NIH may repay eligible student loans up to $10,000 per calendar year, with a $60,000 lifetime maximum, for highly-qualified health-care employees.

Federal Government

The Federal Student Loan Repayment Program authorizes government agencies to set up their own student loan repayment programs to attract or retain highly qualified employees. According to the U.S. Office of Personnel Management, online at **http://opm.gov/oca/pay/studentloan**, government agencies may make payments of up to $10,000 per calendar year and not more than $60,000 total on an employee's FFEL, Direct, Perkins, or Public Health Service loans. Any employee (as defined in 5 U.S.C. 2105) is eligible, excluding those occupying a position excepted from the competitive civil service because of its confidential, policy-determining, policy-making, or policy-advocating nature. An employee receiving this benefit must sign a service agreement to remain in the service of the paying agency for a period of at least three years, and must reimburse the paying agency if he or she leaves employment voluntarily or involuntarily during that period. An employee must maintain an acceptable level of performance in order to continue to receive repayment benefits.

Legal Professions

Relatively low public service salaries prevent many law school graduates with high student loan debt from pursuing public interest careers. The "Higher Education Opportunity Act" of 2008 included a Loan Repayment for Civil Legal Assistance Attorneys program. Borrowers will be required to sign an agreement to remain employed as civil legal assistance attorneys for a required minimum period of three years, unless involuntarily separated from employment. The Department of Education will make payments on behalf of the borrower directly to the loan holder of not more than $6,000 in any calendar year or an aggregate total of $40,000. These benefits will also be offered on first-come, first-served basis and subject to appropriations. Parent PLUS borrowers are not included.

Public service under the Public Service Loan Forgiveness program, which began in 2007 as a result of the College Cost Reduction and Access Act, includes civil legal aid, public defense, and, in addition, all employment by governments and by organizations that are exempt from tax under Sec. 501(c)(3) of the tax law. Borrowers who have made 120 payments as part of the Direct Loan program on or after October 1, 2007 can have the remainder of their federal student loan debt — interest and principal — discharged after ten years of full-time employment in public service. The provisions of this ten-year forgiveness program will assist employers in retaining civil legal aid and criminal indigent defense attorneys.

Are You Ready for an Adventure?

You may not feel ready to launch into a career immediately after graduating from college. Maybe you want to spread your wings and see the world, try something new, or gain some work experience in a particular field to add to your résumé. There are wonderful opportunities that allow you to serve as a volunteer while earning education credits to help pay off your student loans. Some programs entitle you to defer loan payments and earn income, and some pay off a portion of your loans after you complete a certain period of service. Most of these benefits apply only to your federal loans and not to private loans, so be sure to review your loans and make the proper arrangements before committing yourself. You will also be responsible for filling out the necessary applications and forms and requesting that the volunteer program verify your service; this can often be done online.

Many private lenders also grant deferments for periods of volunteer service under recognized programs. You may still be required to make interest payments on unsubsidized or private loans while you are in deferment; you can apply for forbearance or make arrangements for the interest to be paid. If you enter volunteer service right after graduation, while you are still in your grace period, you will not need to make a payment for several months.

AmeriCorps

Every year, AmeriCorps, online at **www.americorps.gov**, offers adults of all ages and backgrounds 75,000 opportunities to serve through a network of partnerships with local and national non-profit groups in the United States. AmeriCorps volunteers tutor and mentor disadvantaged youth, fight illiteracy, improve health services, build affordable housing, teach computer skills, clean parks and streams, manage or operate after-school programs, help communities respond to disasters, and build organizational capacity. AmeriCorps is made up of three major programs: AmeriCorps State and National, AmeriCorps VISTA, and AmeriCorps NCCC (National Civilian Community Corps). AmeriCorps State and National supports a broad range of local service programs that meet critical community needs. AmeriCorps VISTA provides full-time members to community organizations and public agencies to create and expand programs that fight poverty. AmeriCorps NCCC is a full-time residential program for men and women, ages 18-24, who participate in direct, team-based national and community service.

All AmeriCorps programs provide members with a modest living allowance, and some programs provide housing. The National Service Trust provides a Segal AmeriCorps Education Award (AmeriCorps Education Award) of $4,725 for members who successfully complete a year of full-time service in AmeriCorps, and a prorated amount for shorter periods of service. A volunteer can earn up to two awards, for the first two terms of service. The Segal AmeriCorps Education Award can be used to pay education costs at qualified institutions of higher education, for educational training, or to repay qualified federal student loans. The award must be claimed within seven years and can be divided into portions and used at different times. For example, a portion could be applied to existing qualified student loans, and the remainder to tuition at a qualified institution a few years later. The National Service Trust makes payments directly to lenders and educational institutions. Payments made from Segal AmeriCorps Education Awards are considered taxable income in the year that the payment is made to the school or loan holder.

AmeriCorps volunteers qualify for forbearance on government loans during their period of service, and many private lenders will also grant forbearance. If you successfully complete your term, the Corporation for National and Community Service will pay any interest accrued on qualified student loans in forbearance during your AmeriCorps service out of the National Service Trust, regardless of whether the loan is subsidized or unsubsidized, and regardless of the length of time the loan has been in repayment status.

Instead of the Segal AmeriCorps Education Award, AmeriCorps VISTA members may choose to take a post-service cash stipend of $1,200. AmeriCorps VISTA alumni who choose the stipend and have student loans may be eligible for up to 15 percent cancellation on certain types of federal loans.

The College Cost Reduction and Access Act of 2007 (CCRAA) created two new federal programs: a new Public Service Loan Forgiveness program and a new Income-Based Repayment plan (IBR) that helps to make repaying education loans more affordable for low-income borrowers, such as public service workers. If you elect to use the IBR plan, and begin making payments based on your stipend while still an AmeriCorps volunteer, your year(s) of volunteer service will count toward the total of 25 years of payments, after which the remainder of the loan will be forgiven. The stipend is low enough that your IBR payment amount may be $0, which means that interest will continue to accrue on the loan, but if you plan to go into a low-paying career, the benefit might outweigh the extra interest.

The Public Service Loan Forgiveness Program (PSLF) offers forgiveness for outstanding Federal Direct loans for those individuals who make 120 qualifying payments after October 1, 2007 while working full-time in a "public service job." On October 23, 2008, the Department of Education published a final rule that recognizes full-time AmeriCorps service as equivalent to a public service job. If an AmeriCorps volunteer uses an Education Award to make a lump-sum payment on a student loan that is eligible for public service loan forgiveness, the Department of Education will consider that person to have made either (1) the number of payments that would result from dividing the amount of the lump sum payment by the monthly payment amount they would have made under their selected repayment plan; or (2) twelve payments — whichever is less (See 34 CFR § 685.219(c)(2)), toward the 120 payments required for loan forgiveness. The 120 loan payments all have to be made while you are serving in a qualifying public service position, but they do not have to be consecutive. If you anticipate going into public service in the future, pay off one year of your loans at a time instead of using the entire award to make a lump-sum payment so that you receive credit for the maximum number of payments.

Student Conservation Association

Student Conservation Association (SCA) internships (**www.sca. org**) provide opportunities for college and graduate students to learn from resource management professionals, gain tangible skills and experience, and make a substantial contribution to American natural and cultural treasures. SCA Internships are available throughout the year, in all conservation disciplines, and range in length from 12 to 52 weeks. All positions are expense-paid, and most offer travel allowances, housing, insurance, and the same education awards that are available to AmeriCorps volunteers.

SCA members provide crucial conservation services to federal, state, and municipal agencies and private organizations across the U.S., including the National Park Service; The Nature Conservancy; the Bureau of Indian Affairs; AmeriCorps; the U.S. Forest Service; the U.S. Fish and Wildlife Service; the U.S. Geological Survey; U.S. Army, Navy, and Air Force Natural Resource Programs; the Bureau of Land Management; and the National Oceanic and Atmospheric Administration. Many SCA members advance to professional positions with these agencies. The National Park Service estimates that up to 12 percent of its workforce got its start with SCA. Interns work alone and in groups, in urban and wilderness settings, in offices and in the outdoors, in museums, parks, and national lands. You can discover whether you want to pursue a career in conservation or environmental science while paying off a chunk of your federal loans. Deferment and educational award payments do not apply to private loans; you must apply separately for forbearance on your private student loans, and you are responsible for filling out and submitting applications and forms. This can usually be done online. For more information about SCA internships, go to **www.sca.org**, or call 603-543-1700.

CASE STUDY: MY SCA INTERNSHIP WAS A FANTASTIC EXPERIENCE

Momoka, Age 23, SCA Intern

I chose SCA because they offered internships in the visitor centers of National Parks and National Monuments. Honestly, I was also very interested in the free housing. I appreciated the fact that I got to live right on park grounds among the other employees.

I did three different internships with SCA. My first one was an Interpretation / Visitor Services Internship at Tonto National Monument in the central Arizona desert, where I lived in a small caravan overlooking Roosevelt Lake. I welcomed visitors as they came into the visitor center, collected entrance fees, and gave information on the trails. I stood at the ruins and answered visitors' questions. After becoming familiar with the flora, history, and pre-history of the park, I began to give special tours up to a protected ruin site. Since this was a small park, I had the opportunity to try many things. One day, I shadowed a biological technician as he checked on hibernating Gila monsters and snakes. I was so interested in what biological technicians do in the National Parks that I sought an SCA position in the Resource Management department of Canyonlands National Park.

This time, I worked as an assistant for a biological technician. I was thrilled to find out that Canyonlands was part of a group of parks in Southeast Utah. This internship allowed for me to see four different parks! I assisted the biological technician as she surveyed plants in various plots throughout the four parks. A few times, we checked on water quality for year-round springs. We sometimes spent days out in the back country driving on rough roads and camping out in beautiful settings.

My final position was Interpretation / Visitor Services Intern at Natural Bridges National Monument. Tonto National Monument is known for its ruins; Natural Bridges National Monument is recognized for its geology, the highest concentration of natural bridges. Although the internships in these parks required that I do many similar duties, they were very different. At Natural Bridges National Monument, there was a campground with a small amphitheater. I had the opportunity to prepare an evening program to give to visitors in the campground. I also went on "roves," spending hours hiking the trails in the park to check on the condition of the trails and answer questions from any visitors I came across.

Although my three experiences were very different, I loved them all.

I learned that I want to work in the National Park Service, or a similar field. Not only did I get a good feel for how some of the National Parks are run, but I made many friends and acquaintances who have been able to advise me on places to go — since many park rangers have worked at different parks throughout their careers

CASE STUDY: MY SCA INTERNSHIP WAS A FANTASTIC EXPERIENCE

I— and people to contact. The National Park Service can be very competitive, and working with SCA gives you a leg up in the application process and on your résumé.

I recommend SCA to anyone who's interested in working in the National Parks or National Forests. It doesn't matter if you just graduated from high school, are still working on your degree in college, or have just finished college and are looking for something different and exciting to try. There are so many different kinds of internships available and so many different parks and forests to explore. I think everyone can find something they are interested in trying. One warning: check with the park supervisors about the location of the park. Some of these parks can be out in the middle of nowhere. I'm talking about driving hours to get groceries, in some cases! I loved the isolation, and finding myself alone was not a big deal. However, I met some SCA interns who were frantic because there weren't other interns, or people closer to their age, nearby. If you need a social life, be sure to confirm with the supervisor that there are at least two other interns working at the park with you!

I often regretted only spending three months each at these fantastic national parks. During my last month, I kept wishing that I could be there longer. There isn't just one thing that I loved most about my SCA experiences, I loved everything. I saw so many beautiful things and places — I have thousands of pictures to prove it! I made indispensable friendships. I learned so much about the environment, history, pre-history, geology, and most importantly, about myself!

I began my internship while I was still in the grace period for my student loans, and when I finished, I was able to pay off $2,500. That's a good start!

Peace Corps

The Peace Corps (**www.peacecorps.gov**) was established by John F. Kennedy in 1971 to promote better understanding between Americans and the people of foreign countries, and to fill a need for trained men and women in fields such as education, business development, agriculture, health care, information technology, youth outreach, and community development. Peace Corps volunteers commit to 27 months of training and service overseas. Currently, volunteers are serving in 76 countries in Asia, Africa, Europe, the Caribbean, Central and South America, the Middle

East, and the Pacific Islands. To volunteer you must be a U.S. citizen, age 18 years or older. About 95 percent of Peace Corps volunteers have an undergraduate degree, and 11 percent have graduate degrees. Language training is provided when necessary.

Peace Corps Volunteers receive living expenses and transportation to and from the country of service and are given a living allowance that lets them live at a similar standard to the local people in their community, and just over $6,000 at the end of service to help with transition to life in the United States. Volunteers receive two days of vacation for every month of service, a total of 48 days over two years, and many of them use that time to visit nearby countries.

Volunteers may defer repayment of federal Stafford, Perkins, Direct, and consolidation loans during their period of volunteer service and for six months afterwards. Some private student loans may also offer forbearance during Peace Corps service, depending on the terms of the loan contract. Though payment on the loan principal is deferred during the term of service, interest payments must still be made on unsubsidized Stafford Loans, Federal Consolidation Loans that include unsubsidized loans, and Federal Direct Loans. You can apply to your lender for forbearance on interest payments for these loans while you are serving in the Peace Corps, or you may authorize the Peace Corps to make regular interest payments, of up to $168.75 per month, out of your $6,000 readjustment allowance. The Department of Education pays the interest on subsidized Stafford Loans and subsidized Federal Consolidation Loans during the service period. You are responsible to apply to your lender for deferral or forbearance and have the Peace Corps verify your service. Talk to a Peace Corps recruiter to determine the best arrangement for your specific loans.

Like service in AmeriCorps, service in the Peace Corps is recognized as a "public service job" under the Public Service Loan Forgiveness Program (PSLF). Loan payments made using the $6,000 Peace Corps transition allowance, or payments made during the months you are in service, qualify as part of the 120 payments required for loan forgiveness under the program. Peace Corps volunteers who hold Perkins loans are eligible for cancellation of 15 percent of the loan after completing 365 days of service during the first two years of service, and 20 percent after each of the third and fourth years of service. Four full years of service would amount to a 70 percent cancellation of your existing Perkins loan.

CHAPTER 13

Finding a Good Job

The biggest challenge facing new college graduates is finding a job that is personally rewarding and provides enough income to support your life style and pay off your student loan obligations. You may be shocked when you enter the job market and discover the low annual salaries paid for jobs that require considerable training and ability. Unless you are graduating with a degree in computer programming or accounting, you will probably have to enter the lowest-paid levels of a business and "work your way up" by gaining practical experience and compiling a "track record," a process that may take years. You may find that there are few jobs available in your field of study, and that the competition for those jobs is stiff.

Keep Your Goal in Mind

Do not forget why you went to college in the first place. You may encounter discouraging obstacles, or you may be obliged to take a low-paying job just to survive, but do not lose sight of your goals. Success requires effort, investment, and perseverance and is not accomplished overnight. Visualize the future you want for yourself, and identify the steps you must take to achieve it. If you want to pursue a particular type of career, find an entry-level position in that field and begin to learn the business first-hand. Cultivate a network of personal relationships with your bosses and co-workers. Perhaps you will find that you need to go back to school to get a specialized degree or certification to advance your career. Developing a clear mental picture of what you want to achieve will ensure that you continue to make choices and act in a way that moves you in a positive direction.

You may not know exactly what career you want to pursue, but you surely have personal desires and goals. Maybe you have a family and simply want to provide the best possible life for them. You may have a deep personal commitment to your community or the environment. You may want to develop specific talents or personal qualities. Your greatest need may be to establish yourself in a particular town or city so that you can be close to aging parents or family members who need your help. These desires and goals can be a powerful motivation and a guide for career-making decisions.

The important thing is that you do not settle into a groove just because it is comfortable and convenient. It may be necessary to accept a situation for the time being, but do not lose sight of what you really want and need, and keep making effort to achieve your goals.

What Does It Take?

A job search requires the same hard work, thorough research, organizational skills, and time management that got you through your college classes. You will need strategy, organization, and perseverance. The six-month grace period before you begin making student loan payments is intended to allow you time to find employment, but finding a job you want may take much longer. Employment counselors offer a number of statistical formulas, such as "send out 100 résumés to get 3 good job offers," or, "add one month to your job search for every $10,000 of salary." Ideal job offers are few and hard to find, and even after you begin working in one job, you should be developing your résumé and cultivating your skills for future opportunities. Some companies wait weeks and even months before making a hiring decision, and applications and résumés that you send out today may bring results long after you have already started a job somewhere else.

A Good Résumé

Your résumé represents you and determines whether a company is interested in contacting you. A hiring representative is introduced to you through your résumé before he or she meets you in person, so it is crucially important. You can get help writing a good résumé from books, online at sites like **www.Monster.com** and **www.CareerBuilder.com**, and at job service centers and on-campus career centers. Before submitting your résumé for a job, read the job description carefully, and, if necessary, customize the résumé to emphasize the skills and experience that make you a desirable candidate. If appropriate, include non-work experience that demonstrates, for example, your leadership ability or your knowledge of the community. Check and double-check for typographical mistakes and spelling or grammatical errors. Ask two or three friends, or a contact who is experienced in human resources, to read over your résumé and suggest improvements.

Gather examples of your work, photos, writing samples, and written references, and create an approach book or binder, which you can take along to job interviews. Keep a record of your projects and activities. Scan these materials and create a CD or DVD to accompany your résumé.

Create a personal Web site and post your formal résumé, along with any other information that might support your job search, such as references. If you are a web designer, illustrator, engineer, graphic artist, or architect, include samples of your work or class projects. A writer can include writing samples, excerpts, and links to published works. If you are looking for a job in public relations or marketing, include information on projects you have done. Post head shots and action photos, if your personal appearance is important for the job. Include the URL of your site in your written résumé.

Savvy Student Tip:

Be discreet with the information you post about yourself on the Internet. Employers are increasingly looking up the personal profiles of potential job candidates on social networking sites like MySpace and Facebook.
Be careful not to post embarrassing photographs, obscene language, or information about yourself that might be harmful to your job search.

A Good Cover Letter

Your résumé should always be prefaced with a cover letter written specifically for the job you are applying for. Your cover letter can say things that are not expressed in the more impersonal résumé. The cover letter is your sales pitch. It should explain, briefly, how you meet the company's requirements for the job, and how the company might benefit from hiring you.

A Good Job Search

It is a good idea to begin your job search before you graduate. Many schools have placement programs or career centers that connect students with job opportunities. They are staffed with employment counselors who can review your résumé and suggest where to begin looking. Some schools maintain online job placement sites and continue to serve alumni long after they have graduated. Professors and teachers may also be able to recommend job opportunities or provide written references.

The obvious way to begin an online job search is by uploading a résumé and applying for the jobs posted on major job search sites like **www.Monster.com**, **www.CareerBuilder.com**, and **www. Jobster.com**. There are hundreds of specialized sites, such as **www.JournalismJobs.com** and **www.HealthJobsUSA.com**, and sites operated by state, federal, and local agencies, recruiters, and temporary employment agencies. Your application will join hundreds, and even thousands, of others scanned by human resource officers every day, and if you are lucky, you may be contacted to set up an interview. The Internet can be a valuable job search tool in many other ways. Use the Internet to search for companies in the field in which you want to find a job, and visit their Web sites; many of them have online job applications, or give an e-mail or a postal address where you can send a résumé. You can also compile a list of companies in the area where you live and visit each one personally to apply for a job or drop off a résumé. As you do your research, new ideas and opportunities will emerge. Once you are contacted for an interview, you can go online to learn more about a company and to read any news articles that may have been written about it.

You cannot rely on the Internet alone to find a job; many companies hire employees without ever posting a job opening. Personal contact is essential. Visit companies to fill out an application in person. Let everyone know that you are looking for a job: friends, teachers, parents, parents' friends, social contacts, and fellow volunteers. Take on temporary assignments and get to know the employees who work around you. Seek out new relationships by participating in networking groups and committees. Visit state and local job service centers and attend job fairs.

Organizing Your Search

Keep a record of all your job search efforts from the first day. Make a list or spreadsheet with the name and contact information of each company or place where you submitted a résumé, the user name and password (if it is a Web site), and the date. Update the list with any responses, rejections, or interview appointments and their outcomes. Create a file for each company, or give each customized résumé and cover letter a unique name or number and record it on your list.

Keep a sheet of paper with all the information that you use to fill out job applications online. Each time an application form requires you to type additional information, such as a description of your work experience or your personal goals, copy and save it on this sheet. Save time by copying and pasting the information onto future applications. This will also save you from having to retype everything if a form fails to submit correctly.

Savvy Student Tip:

An organized record of your job search is invaluable. Keeping careful records of your job search will not only save you time, but will allow you to review your efforts, identify new possibilities, and have information for future reference. If a company calls you weeks later for an interview, you will have your contact information at hand and be able to review the cover letter and résumé that you sent.

CASE STUDY: FINDING THE RIGHT JOB

Ray Schalk has worked as a recruiter and Human Resources Manager at a transportation company for 18 years.

Devote as much time and effort to your job search as you would to a regular job. If you would normally spend 40 hours a week at work, spend 40 hours a week looking for a job. Don't rely on the Internet. Many young people think they can do everything online; the Internet is just a tool. It doesn't take the place of networking. Present yourself at a company, drop off your résumé, and fill out your application there. Show up in person to ask about job openings.

It is difficult to know whether to take the first offer that comes along, or hold out for a more ideal position. My observation has been that for young people, money is often the primary object. For older, more experienced workers, job satisfaction and quality of life are also very important. For example, jobs that require you to relocate are often more lucrative, but do you really want to uproot yourself and move away from your friends? I like to have weekends to spend with my family. Two things are important to me: the quality of the job, and my quality in doing it. I don't want to be part of a company that provides shoddy goods and services, and I want to feel that I am doing my job well. If money is your only object in taking a job, you may find that the job is not sustainable after a while because it doesn't satisfy the other aspects of your life. How many people have been alienated from their loved ones by their work? It's a familiar plot in movies.

The two most important factors in getting a job are presentation and confidence, the confidence that you can do a good job no matter what kind of work you are assigned. Whomever you work for, the organizational principles are the same. When you are first starting out in the labor market, you don't have experience and expertise; all you have to offer is your willingness to work, your dedication, and

CASE STUDY: FINDING THE RIGHT JOB

your ideas. Come to work on time, be the best you can, do more than what is required of you , set an example, represent the job, recognize other peoples' accomplishments, and respect other people, and you will be appreciated. The company doesn't owe you anything; you are there to learn and gain experience. How you treat your co-workers is very important. As you move up in the organization, respect and recognize everyone, and they will work well with you and for you. Your co-workers are part of your team. When you introduce a co-worker, say, "We work together at…" instead of, "I work with …." It's not "I accomplish," but "We accomplish." In a company, you are not an individual worker; you are a team worker. If you work well with others, you will be picked out for promotion. Have a positive attitude, look for the good side of things, and don't complain. If you don't get that promotion, OK, you tried your best.

There are two signals that it is time to look for another job. One is when your financial realities change and your income is no longer adequate — for example, if you take on a mortgage payment that is higher than the rent you used to pay for an apartment. If there is no possibility for advancement and a raise at your current job, look for a better opportunity. You may feel bad about leaving, but you want to go to a place where you can work harder, and make more money. This may involve additional education, such as getting a certification or a professional degree, and may take some planning. Basically, education equals the opportunity to buy a house. Another signal to leave is when your work environment becomes hostile and you constantly worry about your job. I had a job that I really enjoyed, working with good people in a friendly organization, providing service to the public. Then, the General Manager was fired, and the atmosphere changed completely. His replacement did not set a good example for the rest of the staff, and I knew it was time to go.

It is tough to save money when you have a lot of bills to pay, but setting aside savings is so important. Treat your savings as another bill to pay, and write yourself a check every month. Regard it as an obligation that you owe to yourself and your future. I once advised a friend who complained that he was overwhelmed with bills to pay every month to do this. Years later, he called to thank me — he had been able to retire early because he had established the habit of saving.

Be Flexible

You may inhibit your success in finding a job if you restrict yourself to only one type of job or job title. Be open to opportunities that might be well-suited to your personal abilities, even if they do not correspond to your field of study, or jobs that might teach you new skills. You may need to readjust your job expectations if the job you desire is simply not available.

Online job sites often ask you for a job title or your previous job title, because human resource officers conduct searches by job title. Set up several profiles emphasizing different aspects of your career and using different job titles.

Consider relocating for a good job opportunity, or working overseas for a few years. Expatriate employees often receive benefits such as housing and medical care, travel, and higher salaries to compensate for the hardships of living in a poor country. You may be able to start a career through one of the loan forgiveness programs that discharges federal loans for teachers, medical workers, or public servants in areas of critical need.

What to Do Until You Find It

Until you find a job that fulfills your career goals, you may need to take a temporary job to meet your expenses. This job will also become part of your résumé and work experience, so do your best, and take advantage of every opportunity to develop new skills and professional contacts. Do not let the temporary job become all-consuming and abandon your long-range job search, unless you decide to change course and remain in that job.

If you are unemployed when your grace period ends, or if your salary is not high enough for you to make your scheduled student loan payments comfortably, contact your lender to ask for deferment or forbearance (See Chapter 11:Managing Your Loans) or to arrange for lower payments. Try to pay at least the interest on you loan while you are in deferment or forbearance, to prevent it from being added to the balance of your loan

Savvy Student Tip:

Say goodbye graciously. No employer wants to hire someone who is going to move on as soon as a better offer comes along, but it happens all the time. When you decide to leave a company, comply with company policy in giving advance notice, leaving clear records of your work, and training your successor. If you are unable to give adequate advance notice, discuss this with your employer and offer to help in any way you can. You do not want to leave behind a trail of angry criticism; it could affect your future efforts to find a job.

CHAPTER 14

Making a Budget and Sticking to It

budget is a spending plan that helps you manage your expenses so that they do not exceed your income. The concept of a budget is simple. List all the bills and necessary obligations that you must pay every month, such as rent, utilities, electricity, telephone and payments on loans and debt, and subtract this amount from your total monthly income. The remainder is what you have available to spend on everything else, including food, transportation, clothing, medicine, entertainment, and savings. These expenses can be prioritized; in most cases, food and medicine come before tickets to a basketball game, but transportation might become the top priority if you can not get to work without it. A budget allocates a specific amount for each category. By using self-discipline and sticking to your budget, you can remain in control of your finances and make conscious decisions about your financial goals.

In Chapter 9, you were asked to write down your total income and total expenses for one month. To create a budget, start by writing down everything you have spent over the last month.

Keep all your receipts and invoices in one place. If you use cash, record each amount on a spreadsheet or chart. If you use a debit card all the time, your job will be easier; you can download your bank statement directly or copy and paste it onto a spreadsheet. Some banks include a budget and money management application as part of their online banking services. Assign categories to all your expenses, and in the box next to each amount, put a symbol to show which category it belongs to. Purchases that include items from more than one category — for example, clothing, DVDs and groceries bought at Wal-Mart — will need to be broken down. Remember to include purchases made with credit cards, and the monthly share of any bills that are paid quarterly or semi-annually, such as auto insurance premiums. Total up the amount for each category of expenses, and you will have a picture of your monthly expenses.

Savvy Student Tip:

Keeping an expense record helps you see where all your money is going. It is something like keeping a daily journal of what you eat when you are on a diet. It shows you exactly where your money is going, dispels illusions, and identifies areas where you can make cuts.

Your Expenses

- Review your past month's expenditures and total up the amount for each category. You may be surprised to see how much of your money is going to categories like gasoline or groceries.

- Set target spending amounts for each category, and for any new categories that you would like to add, such as saving for a vacation or a down payment on a house. Remember to include the monthly portion of annual or quarterly expenses, like taxes or auto insurance premiums.

- Find extra money for financial obligations and goals by making cuts in categories of discretionary spending, such as dining out or clothing. Next, look for ways to reduce your expenses in other categories. For example, you could look for a cheaper cell phone plan or eliminate your land line; car pool or organize your errands more efficiently to save on gas; change your grocery shopping habits; or switch to DSL instead of high-speed Internet or a satellite dish instead of cable. Look for ways to lower your energy and utility costs.

- Track your spending in each category, and try to stay close to your target goals. When you find yourself exceeding your target in one area, compensate by cutting down in another.

- Review your budget at the end of every month and plan for the coming month. No two months are alike. Some months will require extra spending for birthdays, holidays, travel, back-to-school supplies, and taxes.

Help with Your Budget

Office supply stores sell home budget books and ledgers that help you record your spending and your target goals for each month. There are also many good books and workbooks that take you step-by-step through the process of creating a budget and offer helpful suggestions along the way.

Personal budget software automates many of the processes of tracking your expenses and incorporates guidelines and financial advice. Data can be imported directly from your online accounts. Your spending patterns are illustrated on graphs and pie charts. Some programs track your spending and show how well you are conforming to your budget. Some even send you alerts when you are close to exceeding your targets. Personal finance software automatically categorizes many of your expenses by using the names of the businesses where you made purchases. You will still need to review the entries and break down purchases that include multiple categories.

YNAB

YNAB (You Need a Budget), online at **www.youneedabudget. com**, is an affordable personal finance software program incorporating a methodology of four simple rules to help you work toward living on your previous month's income and getting out of debt. It can be used in conjunction with a spreadsheet program or as a stand-alone Windows application. You can export information from your online accounts and then import it into YNAB so that the information is housed on your computer and not online

CASE STUDY: YOU NEED A BUDGET

Jesse Mecham is a graduate of the Masters of Accountancy program at Brigham Young University in Provo, Utah, a Certified Public Accountant, and the creator of YNAB and YNAB. Pro, "The Most Effective Money Management System Ever Conceived."

The following is an excerpt from his Web site, **www. YouNeed-ABudget.com:**

"With a new baby in the family and a bit of spare time on my hands during the summer break, I started doing a bit of research about what types of budgeting programs were already out there. We certainly didn't want to be duplicating an idea that was already established. As I tried the various systems, I realized one thing: They were all basically the same. You would enter your income and projected expenses — a static budget. We used a living budget, and I saw that our system was uniquely powerful. This realization helped me find the motivation to begin developing our budget into something that could be used by anyone. The system works. I use it every day (well, a few times per week)."

"… I won't go into all of the details of YNAB Pro, but I'm just glad to see that sticking with the Four Rules of Cash Flow and finding a programmer with a knack for intelligent software design, the money management process has been made even simpler."

Let's talk about these four rules:

1. Stop Living Paycheck to Paycheck

YNAB will require some work on your part — work that will pay big dividends in the future. The methodology and software will help you work toward living on last month's income. What you earn this month, you'll spend the next. Most people take between four and six months to save enough money to live on last month's income. What really matters is that you work toward it.

2. Give Every Dollar a Job

Each month, you'll sit down, with your spouse if applicable, and allocate the funds you have available to your spending/saving categories where they are needed. You'll do this until there are no more available dollars. The process takes 20 minutes and will revolutionize the way you think about your money. Every dollar will be given a job (e.g., rent, car insurance, savings, or Caribbean vacation).

CASE STUDY: YOU NEED A BUDGET

3. Prepare for Rain

Everyone has rainy days. The car insurance is due, you need new tires, the tax man cometh... YNAB will help you anticipate those larger, less frequent expenses. Have an insurance premium due in six months for $600? Stick $100 into your Car Insurance category for each of those months, and watch the balance grow until the bill is due.

4. Roll with the Punches

You will fail. Without a doubt. My wife and I overspend in our grocery category 80 percent of the time. The key is to roll with the punches. YNAB will make small adjustments with that overspending, ensuring that you fix those mistakes before you go on to the next month. You'll barely notice as YNAB makes its gentle corrections.

We are dedicated to providing you with top-notch service — something we're seeing less of these days. Even if you don't purchase YNAB, please learn all you can from the principles taught throughout our site. They will change your life forever.

Get out of debt.

Save for a rainy day.

Live on less than you earn.

Mint.com

Mint.com is a free online budget management tool. It allows you to set up an anonymous account online and automatically imports data from your bank, credit card, home loan, and finance accounts and categorizes your expenses. The information is updated automatically through secure connections to 7,000 banks and financial institutions. Mint's budgeting tools show your average expenditure in each category and help you set goals and track your spending. You can view your balances using your iPhone and set up text message or e-mail messages to alert you when you exceed your budget. Mint.com is funded through targeted advertising; the site identifies credit card offers and other products appropriate for each user.

Quicken

Quicken offers a variety of money management products. Quicken Online, at **http://quicken.intuit.com/online-banking-finances.jsp,** is a free money management tool that gathers information from all your online accounts and organizes it into an overview of your finances. It helps you set budget goals and tracks your spending to help you meet those goals.

Microsoft Money

Microsoft sells two products to help manage your finances and create a budget: Microsoft Money Essentials and Microsoft Money Plus Deluxe. Both allow you to download or import statements from your banking and credit card accounts, show you how your money is being spent, keep track of bills, and generate reports. Microsoft Money Plus Deluxe has additional features that advise you on tax savings, alert you when bills are due, and provide information about your investments. After you import data from your statements, you must edit it to make sure the expenses are allocated to the right categories, a process that can be time-consuming. You can download a free 90-day trial at Microsoft.com (**www.microsoft.com/money**).

ToolsforMoney

ToolsforMoney.com (**www.toolsformoney.com/personal_budget_software.htm**) sells an inexpensive budget tool using Excel spreadsheets. It includes a financial planning tool that projects your family finances far into the future and shows how various circumstances, such as a disability or loss of income, might impact your finances.

Online Banking

If you are not already using online banking, sign up for it. Not only are you able to check your account balances and track your spending almost as fast as it happens, but most banks offer online money management tools that categorize your payments and show you where your money is going, and keep track of all your accounts in one place. Transfers and credit card payments can be made instantly. Online Bill Pay allows you to schedule all your monthly payments in one sitting, and compare the amounts of all previous payments to the same company.

Not the Budget Type?

Keeping to a budget requires commitment, self-discipline, and time to maintain financial records, but the effort pays off in the end. Many people testify to their success in using a budget to control their spending and pay off debts. If you do not have the patience and ability to keep records and track spending month after month, do not abandon the whole idea. There are other, less formal ways to regulate your spending and ensure that you meet your regular financial obligations. Begin implementing some of these now, and you may soon be able to graduate to a complete budget plan.

Review bank and credit card statements regularly.

You should review your bank and credit card statements regularly anyway to protect yourself from theft or fraud. Looking over your income and expenses for every month also makes you aware of how you spend your money. You will be able to identify unnecessary expenses that you can eliminate and see where you are spending too much for particular items. Most online bank statements allow you to click at the top of the column to sort entries alphabetically by payee, so that all your purchases at a single store are listed together and you can see how much you spent for groceries, clothes, and other items.

Pay your bills as soon as you get your pay check.

As soon as you receive income, pay your bills before you spend money for any other purpose. If you use online banking and bill pay, the money will be subtracted from your account balance right away. Next, put a designated amount of money into a savings account. The remainder is what you can spend for everything else.

Deposit your pay check in a savings account.

Deposit your pay check directly into a savings account, and then move money over into your checking account as you need it. Doing this makes you aware of how you are using your money and discourages impulsive and extravagant spending. If your bank charges a fee for a savings account, open a free online savings account with a direct bank, such as Capital One, at **www.capital-one.com/directbanking/online-savings-account/index.php,** or HSBC Direct, at **www.hsbcdirect.com/1/2/1/mkt/savings**. Your money will earn interest while it is in the account.

Use a cash money envelope system.

Stop using a debit card for your everyday expenses. When you receive a pay check, pay your bills and convert the rest into cash. Label a manila envelope for each of your major categories of spending, such as food and household, gas, clothing, entertainment, gifts, and dining out. Allocate the amount of cash you want to use for each category, and put it in the envelope. When all the cash in an envelope has been spent, do not spend any more until your next pay check, or adjust by taking a small amount of cash out of another envelope. Paying in cash rather than with a card is a deterrent to excess spending. Learn more about cash envelope systems at **BlissfullyDomestic.com** or **SoundMoneyMatters.com.**

Marriage and a Family

Budgeting becomes more complicated when you add a spouse and children to a household. Expenses and financial responsibilities increase. You may not want your children to make the same sacrifices that you are willing to make yourself. You no longer have as much control over how money is spent, and there are more emergencies and unexpected expenses. In addition to paying off your student loans, you must now prepare for your children's future education. Two spouses may not agree on financial priorities or share the same attitude toward money. Protect your budget and your family's financial future by reviewing your budget regularly and making adjustments. Win the whole family's commitment to maintaining a budget. Many books and Web sites offer advice about teaching children to manage money. If disagreements over finances threaten to derail your family's financial stability, seek counseling.

Planning for Emergencies and Saving Money

The best way to protect your financial stability is to set aside savings that you can draw on for emergencies. Most financial experts recommend that you save enough to cover your living expenses for six months. Your budget should include a regular contribution, however small, to a savings account that will allow you to pay an unexpected expense without using a credit card or detracting from your other financial obligations.

Many expenses that are labeled emergencies, such as a broken water pipe or a dead car battery, are really part of the cost of maintaining a house or a car. A savings account is one component of a spending plan that covers occasional expenses, such as an automobile repair or a prescription that is not covered by insurance. After you take money out of your savings to pay for a large expense, replenish it by temporarily increasing your monthly contribution.

Whenever you have extra income or leftover cash, add it to your savings account. After your savings account surpasses a target amount, withdraw the excess and apply it to your student loan balance.

Budget Failure

The creation of a successful budget involves trial and error. If your budget plan fails, do not give up. Review your income and expenses, find the source of the problem, and make adjustments for it. Common causes of budget failure include:

- Unrealistic estimated expenses. You may have underestimated how much your groceries cost every month, or not allowed for items like cleaning products and batteries.

- Forgetting to include occasional bills, such as car insurance premiums and property taxes. Money for these expenses should be set aside in monthly increments so that it is available when needed.

Unanticipated purchase of a large-ticket item, such as a television or appliance. If an appliance needs to be replaced because it is broken, this might be treated as an emergency expense. If it is something you want to buy but do not need urgently, save up for it or cut back on another category.

- Excessive spending on gifts or holidays.

- Changes in life style or expenses. These changes could be seasonal and temporary, such as heating costs in winter, or permanent, such as a new job that entails driving longer distances every day or a teenaged child getting a drivers license.

- Inadequate income. When your income is not enough to cover your monthly expenses, you need to increase your income or take steps to cut your expenses. This might include moving to a less expensive apartment, canceling your cable television, selling a car, or dropping a gym membership. If you have not already done so, switch to a graduated or income-based repayment plan for your student loans.

CHAPTER 15

Making the Most of Your Money

Keeping Off the Plastic

If you cannot pay off the balance on your card by the end of the month, it is better not to use a credit card to make a purchase. The interest charges on that purchase may end up costing you twice what you paid for the item itself. Always look for another way of paying for something. Incurring more debt should be a last resort.

Used responsibly, credit cards are convenient for certain purposes, such as providing a backup for emergencies. A credit card account may help to establish your credit history. Credit cards are also helpful when you want to rent a car or reserve a hotel room. There are other ways to manage these situations, including building up savings as an emergency fund and building up your credit history with a student loan or an auto loan.

CASE STUDY: TIPS FOR GETTING THE MOST VALUE OUT OF A CAR

Felipe DeLaPlaza is an engineer with 25 years of experience working with cars.

Always buy a used car. It's foolishness to buy a new car. Someone who has a lot of money available and wants to buy a new car doesn't care how much it costs. It's just caprice; he wants the latest model. Buy a used car, but one that is still fairly new with as few miles as possible, say 30,000 to 60,000. You need a car; you don't need a new car.

It is best to buy a used car directly from the owner. He has driven it for a few years, bought another new car, and now he needs to sell this one. It is hard to sell, and he's willing to let it go for the best offer. He just needs to sell it and get it out of his driveway or garage, where it is losing value as it sits. A used car dealer or a middleman is in no hurry to sell; if you don't buy it, somebody else will. If the sticker price is $6,000, you might be able to get a dealer down to $5,800. But if you go up to a private owner and tell him you only have $3,000 in your pocket to buy his car, he'll take the offer rather than lose the opportunity to get rid of the car.

When you're shopping for a used car, look at the mileage first. Ask to see the owner's maintenance records — if the oil has been changed every 3,000 miles and the car has been serviced regularly, the engine will be in good condition. Look at the transmission fluid. On an automatic transmission, it should be clear and pink. Even dark pink is OK if it is clear and beautiful. If the transmission fluid is brown or dark brown, don't buy the car. Check that both the tank and the radiator are full of coolant. A fishy smell just means the coolant is old; it can be changed. Never buy a car with "extras" — no racer rims on the wheels, no headers, no modifications to the engine, nothing special. Everything should be original, just like it came from the dealership. Everything should be OEM — from the original equipment manufacturer.

Try to buy from a responsible owner. Never buy a car from a teenager. A teenager has probably driven it like a race car, after going to the movies and watching The Fast and the Furious.

Among used cars, go with the "Three Musketeers:" Honda, Toyota, and Nissan. You will have a much higher probability of getting value for your money. You could also try the "d'Artagnans:" Mazda, Suzuki, Isuzu, and Mitsubishi. Even if the mileage is up to 80,000 or 90,000, you still have a lot of car left. When the mileage is over 90,000, make sure the car has a new timing belt. If the timing belt breaks while you are driving, you'll need a head job.

Cars are made perfect; their owners and mechanics break them. Change the oil regularly. Once a week, check all your fluids: coolant, transmission, brake fluid,

CASE STUDY: TIPS FOR GETTING THE MOST VALUE OUT OF A CAR

and power steering. If a fluid level is low or the fluid is discolored, it's a sign that something is wrong. Check the air pressure in your tires. It only takes 15 minutes on a Sunday to check over your car. As long as an engine has enough oil and enough coolant, it will never break.

Do You Really Need That Flat Screen TV?

You have grown up watching television commercials and looking at magazine ads in which suave, elegant men and women get in and out of luxury sedans and flash expensive gold watches and diamond jewelry. You know that they are actors, not real men and women, and that the automakers and jewelers are simply trying to engage your emotions and make you want to buy their products. So why buy into the myth? Do you really believe that owning a particular make of automobile makes a person smarter, stronger, richer, or better? You might have a deep admiration for something , but is buying it going to change who you are in any way? When you are tempted to buy an expensive item, stop and ask yourself, "Why do I want to buy this? Is this something I really need? Is this really important?" Never make a big-ticket purchase on impulse, or because it is a good deal, or because "the sale ends today." Distance yourself and take time to consider the consequences of buying something you cannot afford. How will this purchase affect your financial situation? How long will it take you to pay for it? Are you going to come up short when it's time to pay for necessary expenses?

If, after serious consideration, you decide you have to have the awesome new computer that will be the envy of all your friends, or the Movado watch that will impress everyone at the office, look for the cheapest way to get it. Compare prices online and find the best deal. Can you buy it second-hand or refurbished? Could you return it for a refund if you discover after a day or two that it doesn't mean so much to you after all? Car dealerships often have new-model cars that were leased for a few months and returned in almost-pristine condition. Refurbished cameras and game consoles come with warranties from the manufacturer and cost a fraction of the price of new merchandise.

Before adding a few hundred more dollars to your credit card debt, or spending your entire tax refund, figure out how you are going to accommodate this big bite out of your finances. Can you make up the difference by sacrificing something else, like a vacation trip? Is there some way you can generate extra income, such as a garage sale or a freelance gig, to pay for it all at once? If you put this money toward paying off your existing debt, how much money would you save yourself in the long run?

Smart Shopping

You can buy everything you need, and still stay within your budget, if you know when, where, and how to shop. You may already know how to get the best deals on some things, like cell phone plans or cameras, and you can apply similar tactics to almost everything else. In today's difficult economy, newspapers and magazines are full of useful tips. Learn from your friends; those computer whizzes at your office can tell you how to get a bargain on a laptop, and your next door neighbor might know where you can buy a new car battery and get it installed for free.

Your newest ally is the Internet, an endless source of information and your gateway to a world of discounts. If you already know what you want to buy, look it up on the Internet to compare prices and find a location near you where it is being sold. If you have seen something you want in a store, go online to see what other types and brands are available, how they compare with each other, and where you can get the best price. Need an external hard drive? Do some research and read the users' comments so that you know which one suits your purpose best. Even if you make the actual purchase in a local store, you will go in armed with an understanding of what you are buying and will not be talked into spending more than you need to. The Internet is also a good way to locate specialty or hard-to-find items, such as replacement parts for computers or backpacking equipment that might be overpriced or not available locally.

Numerous Web sites post information about discounts, coupons, and promotional offers, including the weekly ads from newspaper inserts. Before heading out the door with your wallet, check to see whether there is some way to get a discount on your favorite brand, or if a local electronics store is having a big sale. When you receive special offers in the mail or cut coupons out of magazines, pop them into a file folder for future use. Each discount might seem small by itself, but if you can shave a few dollars off of every oil change and hair cut, the savings add up.

Clothing

It is time to stop wandering aimlessly through the aisles of clothing stores, trying on whatever catches your eye and buying everything you fall in love with, regardless of the price. Shop with a purpose; if you need a new sweater, go straight to the sweater department and look for the "Sale" signs. Before you start examining sweaters, fix the amount you want to spend in your mind, and do not even consider anything costing more than your limit. You may be forced to rearrange your budget when you see how much sweaters actually cost, or find that good quality is slightly more expensive than you thought, but at least you are making a conscious decision and not one driven by impulse.

If your friends ask you to accompany them to the mall, leave your credit card at home and take only as much cash as you can afford to spend. Enjoy browsing and window shopping; if you come across something that you really want, you can come back and purchase it later, after you have given it some thought.

Wardrobe Essentials

Your wardrobe does not have to be a large one if it contains the items you need. Give priority to the clothes you need for work every day. Everyone needs at least one suit or "dress-up" outfit, including a respectable pair of shoes, to wear for job interviews and special occasions. You might spend a little more for this outfit because you need to feel confident wearing it. Take time to find clothes that flatter you. If something does not fit you well, has to be constantly readjusted, or shows too much cleavage, do not buy it. Stay away from flamboyant, unforgettable colors or features such as large collars that might be in style this season but will be dated six months from now. Store your "good" outfit neatly in your closet and keep it for those special occasions when you need to look your best. If you dress up for work, change into something casual as soon as you get home, and put your good work clothes away to avoid staining or damaging them. Take care of your clothes and shoes so that they remain wearable and do not need to be replaced for a long time.

Once your essential wardrobe is established, you can start spending money on other, less necessary items, such as workout clothes and casual clothing. When you have the everyday clothing you need, you can indulge in "fun" outfits that you might wear only a few times.

Where, When, and How to Save Money on Clothes

Never pay retail prices for clothing, except as a last resort, such as when you cannot find a necessary item anywhere else, or when you have to wear the newest style of jacket to impress your clients. Most clothing stores regularly hold sales in which they discount items just a few weeks after they appear on the racks. At the end-of-season clearance sales, shoes and clothes are marked down to as little as 25 or 30 percent of their original price. Wait until after the clearance sales begin to shop at your favorite department store, and look for additional discount coupons in their weekly ad brochures. Swimwear goes on sale after mid-summer. Evening dresses are half-price or less when the local high-school proms are over.

If you want to wear the newest styles and do not want to pay department-store designer prices, you will find lower-priced knockoffs in brand stores and in large retail stores like Sears and Target. Your favorite brand names are affordable in discount retailers such as Marshall's, Ross, Burlington Coat Factory, T.J. Maxx, Men's Wearhouse and Bealls, or in outlet malls where brand-name goods are often sold for half of their original prices.

Are you living in Florida and planning a midwinter visit to New York or a snowboarding trip to Utah? Ask around; you may be able to borrow warm clothing from a friend or co-worker. If you need formal wear for a one-time event, such as a friend's wedding, consider renting it. Consignment stores carry expensive gowns that have been worn only once or twice, as well as suits and elegant dresses. Thrift stores and second-hand stores are good places to look for work pants and denim jackets, vintage clothing, and one-of-a-kind T-shirts.

Some companies offer a clothing subsidy to employees who must buy expensive clothes for jobs that entail meeting with clients or speaking in public. If you are obliged to spend a substantial amount on clothing to meet company dress standards, ask your boss whether such a policy exists.

Food and Pharmacy

Keep It Simple

Try not to buy more food than you need; if you find yourself regularly throwing out rotten vegetables and stale cereal, cut back on the amount you buy every week. Keep meat and bread in the freezer if you are not going to eat it right away. Do not cook more than you can eat in a single meal, unless you are going to package up the leftovers and eat them for lunch the next day. Leftover food can also be frozen and kept for an occasion when you are hungry and do not have time to cook. Every few weeks, skip a trip to the grocery store and use up the food items you already have in your pantry and refrigerator. If you find yourself consistently buying too much food and wasting it, retrain yourself by planning your menus for a week and buying only what you need for those meals.

Stick to basic ingredients; prepared and pre-packaged foods typically cost two to three times more and often contain sodium, sugar, and preservatives that are harmful to your health. Use meat in small quantities as part of a stir fry, stew, or pilaf. Prepare vegetarian meals several times a week, and use lentils and beans, which are inexpensive but nourishing

If you are following a recipe that calls for small quantities of costly spices, cheeses, nuts, and other ingredients that you don't already have, look for less expensive substitutes, and leave out those that are not essential. Tailor your menus around the spices and condiments that you have on hand. Substitute cheaper cuts of meat and less expensive wines.

Keep It Cheap

Buy your staples in discount supermarkets, and shop in more expensive markets only for special ingredients and unique items, such as bakery goods. Local produce, fish, and meat are typically cheaper in ethnic grocery stores or farmers' markets.

Take advantage of weekly supermarket specials, two-for-the-price-of-one offers, and the sale items that are often displayed on end caps. Look for "cookie wars" and "cereal wars" in which well-known brands drastically lower their prices for a week or two. Buy food that has nutritional value; avoid expensive snacks like potato chips and cookies.

Look for produce in season, and keep your purchases within a specific price range. Frozen vegetables and fruits are reasonably priced, and may be more nutritious than their fresh counterparts because they are harvested when they are ripe.

Memberships in wholesale clubs, like Sam's Club, Costco, and BJ's, can save you money if you shop carefully. Split the cost of buying large quantities with a friend or neighbor; do not buy large amounts of anything unless you will use it. Some communities operate food co-ops — membership organizations that lower the cost of food by buying in bulk at wholesale prices.

Coupons can save you money, as long as you use them to purchase the products that you would buy anyway. If you are required to buy two or three of something in order to use the coupon, you may find you are spending more than you intended and overstocking your pantry with supplies that may still be there a year later. You can search for coupons online at sites like CoolSavings (**www.coolsavings.com**), Grocery Coupon Network (**www.grocerycouponnetwork.com**), Entirely Coupons (**www.entirelycoupons.com**), and Coupon Share (**www.couponshare.com**).

Buy Generic

Generic products often sit on the shelf side-by-side with their more expensive brand name counterparts and cost significantly less. If you have any doubts, pick up both packages and compare the ingredients. Buy store-brand and generic products whenever they are available.

Pharmacists are required by law to offer generic drugs, if they exist, in place of more expensive drugs. If the pharmacist who is filling your prescription suggests a generic drug, take it. When paying for a prescription, be sure you are using any insurance benefit or discount program to which you are entitled, including AAA (American Automobile Association). Some pharmacies offer a range of prescription drugs at a single low price.

Calculate the Trade-Offs

A British economist recently suggested that working people should calculate the value of their time by estimating how much they would earn per hour if they were doing household chores like cooking and cleaning for a salary. Seen in those terms, the two hours you spend preparing a meal in the kitchen and cleaning up afterwards, plus the cost of ingredients, might add up to more than the cost of dining in a moderately-priced restaurant. If you could be earning money doing something else with that time, or if you are exhausted from working hard and need some rest or exercise, it sometimes makes economic sense to eat out, or buy take-out food. There may even be enough leftovers for another meal. On the other hand, unless you are careful, a steady diet of restaurant food is likely to make you overweight and unhealthy. Not everything can be measured in dollars and cents. In order to work productively, and continue to sustain your productivity, you must take care of your physical, social, and psychological needs. Successful money management means making choices that contribute positively to your life, without straying outside of your budget.

Cleaning Products

Sophisticated cleaning products are expensive, perhaps because their manufacturers spend so much on television advertising. Time-tested cleaning products like baking soda, bleach, and ammonia cost little and do an excellent job in the bathroom and kitchen. A floor cloth does a better job washing a tile or linoleum floor than a mop. You can find tips on household cleaning online. While some products are worth the money you pay for them, many can be easily replaced with a simpler alternative. Supplies like sponges, buckets, brooms, and mops are often sold in dollar stores.

Big-Ticket Items

The purchase of items like computers, cameras, furniture, musical instruments, appliances, carpets, MP3 players, and cell phones that are going to cost $100 or more demands some consideration. By doing research before you rush out to buy them, you can be assured that you are getting value for your money and not being overcharged.

Check Prices in at Least Three Stores

Do not make any decisions until you have checked prices from at least three different vendors. You can do this by searching online and by visiting the stores in your area where the item is sold. Why does one model cost more than another? Does it have special features that the other does not have? Is a store offering a special promotion? Are there delivery or shipping costs or installation fees? How long before you receive the item? Is there a warranty? Sometimes, a model that is about to be discontinued is discounted, and you can get extra features for less than the price of a much simpler new model. After doing your research, you will have a good grasp of the product and be able to make an informed choice.

Electronics stores often entice buyers by offering substantial mail-in rebates or "free" add-ons. They know that only 4 percent of the people who purchase these items are going to complete the rebate process. If you are tempted by one of these offers, apply for the rebates immediately, and deposit the rebate checks as soon as you receive them; many of them expire after 90 days. Do not throw out the packaging material, because most rebates require the original UPC bar code to be cut out of the box and mailed in. Follow the instructions on the rebate form to the letter, and save copies of all your rebate forms and paperwork until after you have received your rebate check.

Liquidators and Outlets

The principle is not necessarily to buy the cheapest item, but to get good value for your money. A cheap computer may not have enough memory for your needs, and a cheap washing machine or refrigerator may use more electricity and break down three years sooner than a more expensive one. Look for discounted prices on better-quality items at outlets, "ding-and-dent" sales, and liquidation stores. You may be able to buy a sophisticated, quality appliance with a scratch on it for the same price as a much cheaper basic model. Sometimes you can purchase a model that has been on display for less than one that has never been taken out of the box. A furniture liquidator offers brand-name furniture at low prices, but sells only what is on display in the store.

Shop the Classifieds

You may be able to locate good-quality used furniture or appliances for a fraction of what you would pay for something new by looking at classified ads in your local newspaper or on Web sites like Craigslist.com. You may have to pay in cash and provide transportation; you can rent a truck by the hour from a home improvement store. By buying used furniture and appliances, you postpone making a big outlay for several years, until you are better able to afford it.

Buy IKEA

If you cannot find what you want in the classifieds, furnish your home or apartment with low-cost furniture and fittings that you assemble yourself. IKEA is famous for its business model, selling and shipping everything in flat boxes and passing savings on to consumers. Stores like Wal-Mart, Kmart, Target, and home improvement and office supply stores sell unassembled furniture at low prices. Often, this furniture costs less than you would pay for wood and raw materials to make your own shelves or tables.

Amazon.com, Overstock.com, Buy.com, and eBay.com

Take advantage of liquidations, closeouts, and tax sales by shopping online at Web sites like **Amazon.com**, **Overstock.com**, **Buy.com**, and **eBay.com**. Items on sale may be shipped free of charge, and you will find a wide range of qualities and prices to select from.

Travel and Vacations

Vacations and travel are enriching and bring families closer together. It is not necessary to spend much money in order to have a relaxing, meaningful travel experience.

Take Short Trips and Stay Close to Home

Calculate how much you will need to spend per day for lodging, food, and entertainment, and take short trips of three or four days. By staying close to home, you will save money on gas and travel, and have more time to spend at your destination. Whether you go to a lake, the mountains, the beach, a historical city, or a country music festival, three days is long enough to make it a real break from routine. Fun does not have to have a high price of admission. Spend a few days doing something you enjoy, such as camping, sailing, fishing, canoeing, skiing, sketching, looking for fossils, or visiting museums.

Look for Promotions and Special Offers

If you can travel during the off-peak season, or during the week, you may be able to avail yourself of promotional offers designed to fill empty hotel rooms and airline seats. You may find an all-inclusive package or a cruise that is within your budget. Be sure to ask whether there are extra charges. Many time-share companies offer a short stay in return for your participation in a sales presentation; there are age and income restrictions. If you see an inexpensive air fare to a particular city, plan your vacation around that destination.

Always check with the local Visitors Bureau to see whether they have a hotel discount program or specials for walk-in visitors. Some Visitors Bureaus offer discounted tickets for theater shows or theme parks, and the staff can give advice on how to economize during your stay. Look for hotel coupons on Web sites like **www.discounthotel.com** and **www.roomsaver.com**. Use AAA and travel rewards programs. Check the hotel's own Web site, or call reservations to ask for their best available rate.

Stay with Relatives and Friends

Visit friends or relatives and stay in their homes. You will have an opportunity to see the area from the viewpoint of someone who lives there and knows it well, and renew your relationships at the same time.

Save on Food

Look for hotels that offer a free breakfast. Eat one restaurant meal per day and fill in with simple snacks or inexpensive fast food. Many well-known restaurants offer a business lunch or, in some areas, an "early bird" dinner at a discounted price. Take advantage of happy hours and hospitality nights. If you decide to splurge, take your time, make the most of it, and have a memorable evening.

Air Fares

At certain times of the year, for brief periods, air fares to Europe or Asia are much lower than usual, and cruises are discounted as ships are repositioned between seasons. If you are interested in traveling abroad, tell your travel agent, and sign up for e-mail alerts on travel Web sites. Look for travel agencies that specialize in certain destinations; for example, an Asian travel agent may leave business cards in a Chinese grocery store or restaurant, or advertise in an Asian newspaper.

Look for promotions such as companion fares for family and friends. If you have a credit card that offers travel rewards, or have accumulated frequent flier miles, use them. If you have to make sudden travel plans to attend the funeral of a close family member, ask the booking agent about bereavement fares; you will need to produce proof, such as a copy of the death certificate.

Travel search engines such as **CheapTickets.com** and **Kayak.com** search multiple Web sites for the lowest airfares. Do not forget to check the airline's Web site for special offers. If you are flexible about your travel dates, you will be able to use the lowest possible fare. **Hotwire.com** offers very low prices, but you do not learn the details, such as the airline or hotel, until after you have paid. **Priceline.com** allows you to "name your own price" and see whether an airline or hotel accepts it.

Rent an Apartment or a Home

If you are traveling with a group, you can save money on food and accommodations by renting an apartment or a home. Web sites like **rentalo.com** and **VRBO.com** connect you with private-ly-owned homes, condos, and apartments whose owners may be willing to rent to you for a short stay. You can save money by preparing simple meals in a kitchen instead of eating in restaurants. If you live near a popular travel destination, you may even be able to trade homes with someone from another country.

Create Your Own Itinerary

Instead of paying big bucks for a guided tour, consult some of the many travel guides and Web sites for do-it-yourself travelers and plan your own itinerary. These guides will tell you what to expect, where to stay, where to go, and how to get there. You will experience the culture of an area more directly by finding your own way around. Many regions have rail passes or travel passes that allow you to travel as much as you want during a specific time period, for a single price. Consider staying in a youth hostel or renting a room in someone's home.

Gifts

Buying gifts for birthdays, baby showers, weddings, and holidays can be a substantial expense, but it is a social convention that is difficult to ignore. Gift giving is a way of affirming social relationships, showing appreciation, or simply showing that you care for someone. Set aside a small part of your budget for buying gifts. Do not forget the real significance of a gift: that you have taken the time to remember someone and try to please them.

Before shopping for a gift, set a mental limit on the amount that you are going to spend, and stick to it. Your best friend may deserve a Gucci hand bag, but since you cannot afford it, buy something within your budget, but equally luxurious, such as a box of good chocolates. For a baby shower at the office, suggest that everyone make a fixed contribution to buy one large gift or a gift basket. For a child, avoid the latest (expensive) electronic game and give a hands-on toy, such as a soccer ball or art supplies; it is likely to be just as exciting and provide hours of absorbing play.

Christmas holiday shopping can break your budget and set you behind for several months if you are not careful. The holiday décor and music evokes a flood of emotions and childhood memories that may cause you to get carried away and make purchases you would never make in January. Make a list of the people you want to buy a gift for, and decide how much you can afford to spend. Include incidentals like Christmas decorations and cookie ingredients in your budget. Decide which things are important to you and which things you can forego. Buy gift wrap in the dollar stores. Avoid wandering through crowded stores full of impulse items. Look online for price breaks and inexpensive but appropriate gifts. Your friends do not want you to go bankrupt; search for a (gently) used book or DVD online that has special meaning, or make a batch of cookies or fudge. If you need a last-minute gift, Christmas merchandise, like boxed gift sets, is often sold half-price a day or two before Christmas. Do not buy a gift that you know will never be used by the person receiving it. Most of all, think about how you will feel in mid-January, when you are looking at the consequences of your generosity. If gift-giving will leave you feeling regretful, do not do it.

> **Savvy Student Tip:**
>
> *Use your iPhone to stay on track. For $4, you can get the iPhone application Gift List Budget Shopper (**http://appshopper.com/productivity/gift-list-shopper**), which keeps track of your gift list as you shop and alerts you when you are exceeding your budget. You can e-mail your gift spending records as a spreadsheet to import into Excel or your budget software.*

Do It Yourself

You can save yourself several hundred dollars per year by mowing your own lawn, shampooing your own carpet, washing your own windows, detailing your own car, and doing your own pest control. Your investment of time and labor not only cuts household expenses, but keeps you active and gives you a sense of accomplishment and self-sufficiency. Most equipment comes with detailed instructions; if you have questions, ask a neighbor for help or look online.

These days, a service call from a repairman can easily cost over $100, and that does not necessarily include parts and additional labor. When the water will not drain out of your washing machine, the lights go out in the living room, your computer is acting funny, or the refrigerator is not cold any more, use your common sense and try to figure out what is wrong before you call a professional. The solution might be as simple as removing a CD from a disc drive, resetting a fuse, or defrosting the freezer drain. There are often a few simple tests you can do yourself that will rule out or diagnose common problems.

Online, you can find instructions and diagrams that show you how to do almost everything, and tips to help you identify the problem. Web sites of home improvement stores and auto parts stores have "how to" sections. Try sites like **Howto.com** and **Fix-it.com**, or just type a few words describing your problem in the search box. Ask a knowledgeable neighbor or relative for advice. After you have reviewed information from several sources, you will have a better understanding of the available options. If you do need to call a professional repairman, you will know what he or she is talking about and whether you are being overcharged or talked into unnecessary repairs. Some things, like electrical wiring, are best done by a licensed professional who knows local building codes and has the right tools for the job. Get at least three quotes for a job and compare the services being offered. Ask for references if the job is going to cost much.

If you have a neighbor who has all the right tools and knows how to do repairs, ask for help in exchange for a service that you can offer, such as setting up a home computer network, pet-sitting during a vacation, catering a birthday party, altering clothes, or tutoring a child. If you cannot offer anything in exchange, offer to pay cash.

Insurance

Insurance is protection. You pay a monthly, quarterly, or annual amount (premium) to an insurance company in exchange for a guarantee that if you suffer an accident, loss, or major medical expense, the company will compensate you for most of the costs. If you are not adequately insured, you risk not only your own financial future, but that of your family. A single unexpected mishap could leave you homeless, without a car, owing a huge sum in medical bills or damages, or, worst of all, disabled and unable to earn a living. Insurance is a necessary part of your budget. One aspect of achieving financial stability is understanding the type of insurance you hold, getting the best price for your insurance, and making the most of your insurance benefits.

Shop Around

Get quotes from at least three insurance agents or companies before buying any kind of insurance. The insurance market is competitive, and there can be a considerable difference in the prices charged by different companies. You can find local insurance agents through your telephone directory or Better Business Bureau. Many insurance companies offer online quotes or live chats with agents. Be sure to give exactly the same information to each company, and compare the details of the coverage offered under each policy. Web sites like **netQuote.com** and **Insure-Compare-Save.com** allow you to compare quotes from different insurance companies online.

Automobile Insurance

If you own an automobile, you are legally required to have automobile insurance. Many factors influence the amount of your monthly premium, including your age, gender, driving record, credit score, type of vehicle, presence of anti-theft devices, and whether you have been in an accident during the past three years. Insurance companies use statistics to determine the premiums they charge. Insurance premiums for sports cars are higher because the drivers are more likely to drive recklessly, and for SUVs because they are more costly to repair and cause more damage in an accident. When you are shopping for a car, choose one that costs less to insure.

Some insurance companies offer a "good student discount" for high-school and college students with a certain grade point average, and for drivers who have taken additional driving classes. You can also get a discount if you have more than one vehicle insured with the same company.

Lower your monthly premium by raising your deductible — the amount you must pay out of pocket for repairs or medical expenses if you have an accident.

Select only the coverage you need. If you are driving an old car that is already paid for, you can lower your premium by removing collision damage from your policy. When repairs to a car cost more than the car is worth on the market, the insurance company will write it off and pay only the car's current market value.

Homeowners or Renters Insurance

Homeowner's and renter's insurance pays for repairs when your home is damaged, but it may also cover liability if someone is injured at your home and for replacing stolen property. Read your policy carefully and understand exactly what is covered. You can lower the premium for homeowners insurance by raising the deductible, but you will pay more out of pocket if anything happens to your home. Do not use the insurance unless you need to, as excessive claims will raise the premium or cause the insurance company to drop you. Ask your agent what items of personal property are covered by the policy, and inquire about insuring valuables, such as jewelry, art, and musical instruments.

Health Insurance

It can be difficult to maintain health insurance coverage while you are starting a career, temporarily unemployed, or moving from one job to the next. According to the U.S. Census, about one-third of young adults between the ages of 20 and 30 did not have health insurance in 2007. Health insurance is typically offered through employers, but many young people turn down health insurance coverage because they feel the premiums are unaffordable on their low starting salaries, and because they do not understand the financial risks of not being insured. If you are offered health insurance through your employer, try to take advantage of it. Read the literature, ask questions, and be sure you understand the available options and the benefits you will receive. Some companies offer choices; you can choose a higher deductible and pay lower monthly premiums, or you may be able to opt for a cheaper managed-care plan. Most insurance has a deadline requiring you to enroll within a certain number of days after you begin working for a company — don't miss out by procrastinating.

Some states have enacted legislation raising the age at which dependant young adults are dropped from their parents' insurance policies. You may be covered as long as you are in school, unemployed, or supported by your parents.

The cost of private health insurance is likely to be prohibitive, but there are several types of alternative health insurance that can help you maintain at least some coverage. Short-term health insurance and short-term major medical insurance are offered by several insurers. Short-term major medical insurance costs from $75 to $100 per month and will cover your expenses in case of an accident or serious illness. Short-term insurance can be purchased one month at a time for up to twelve months.

Members of Hostelling International (**www.hihostels.com**) get a 10 percent discount on travel, backpacking, and adventure travel insurance (**www.columbusdirect.com/Travel-Insurance**), which covers medical expenses as well as loss, theft, and legal expenses during long trips.

CHAPTER 16

Adding to Your Income

You have done everything you can do to minimize the interest rate on your student loans, and have stabilized your financial situation so that you are able to make your monthly loan payments and take care of your living expenses without going into a state of emergency every three or four months. Now it is time to think about accelerating your loan payments. The sooner you pay off your student loans, the sooner you will have additional resources to direct toward other areas of your life. Previous chapters have discussed how to make the most of the income you have by reducing expenses. Now we are going to look at ways of adding to that income. If you can generate additional income, and use some of it to pay down the principal of your student loans, you will not only pay off your loans sooner and save yourself thousands of dollars in interest, you will establish a pattern of behavior that will allow you to achieve other goals.

Your primary source of income is probably your job, but do not limit yourself to the field in which you are employed. You are surrounded by opportunity. Be flexible and creative in putting your talents to use. If you actively seek additional sources of income, you will gradually develop other areas of your life, and you may even find new avenues of success.

Your Job

The best opportunity to negotiate a good compensation and benefits package is when you sign on with a company. Research the salaries of other workers in the same field and geographical region, and ask for similar compensation. Read the materials given to you by the human resources office and ask questions. Know what benefits are being offered, such as health insurance, paid vacation and sick days, discounts on merchandise or services, and 401(k) or pension plans, and make use of them. Find out whether the company participates in any programs to forgive or pay off student loans.

The first place to look for additional income is from the job you already have. You do not want to jeopardize your employment by asking for a raise when times are difficult, but if you believe you genuinely deserve more compensation because of the type of work you are doing, because you are shouldering more responsibility, or because someone else in the same position is being paid more than you, you are justified in asking. Make an appointment to speak to your boss or your human resources officer, and come prepared to make your case. Document the work you are doing, and give examples of how your efforts have benefited the company. If a raise is not immediately forthcoming, ask what you can do to merit one.

Learn as much as you can about your company's compensation policies without being indiscreet. You may be able to enter a higher salary range by obtaining a professional certification or getting another degree. Some companies offer scholarships or tuition for employees who attend classes related to their work.

Reducing Tax Withheld from Your Paycheck

Are you due a substantial refund when you file your taxes? It is exciting to receive a large tax refund once a year, but that same money might serve you better if you receive it in the form of a slightly larger paycheck every two weeks. Fill out a new W4 form and give it to your employer to reduce the amount of tax being withheld from your paycheck. You can find a W4 form on the IRS Web site, at **www.irs.gov/pub/irs-pdf/fw4.pdf.**

Identify Your Resources

Your education and professional training are not your only personal resources. What other experience have you gained during your life? What are your talents and hobbies? Are you outgoing and a good public speaker? Are you an introverted writer? You may be able to put your abilities to work to increase your earning power. If you are good at a particular sport, you can coach a team or instruct an evening class. An artist can put some of his or her work up for sale in a gallery or rent a space at a weekend art festival. A good cook can cater for parties or decorate birthday cakes. A musician can accompany performers at local clubs. Even if activities like these are not immediately lucrative, it is important to start them, gain experience, and give them time to develop. Your extracurricular activities also bring you into contact with new people who may be able to help you in other ways.

Your friends and family are another valuable resource. A friend or family member who already has a successful sideline can teach you the business and help you get started. Maybe you have a contact who can help you get supplies, or wholesale prices on an item that you can sell for a profit. Friends and family members can help to spread the word and find new customers or clients.

Your computer can be used to enhance your income in many ways, whether you use it to do work, advertise a business, sell something, network with colleagues, or conduct research. You may own other equipment or property that you can rent out or use to earn extra income, such as a pressure washer, paint sprayer, or snow blower. If you own professional-quality camera equipment or audio-visual equipment, offer your services at sporting events or celebrations, or create images and videos to sell online.

Moonlighting and Freelancing

Moonlighting is the practice of working a second job outside of your regular hours of employment. Some moonlighting is an extension of existing employment, such as an off-duty policeman who provides security for a private event, a medical resident who staffs a clinic outside of working hours, a lawyer who serves on an advisory board, or an accountant who teaches business classes at a university. Companies may provide opportunities for their employees to "moonlight" when there is extra work to be done. Moonlighting can also be work done on your own behalf, but related to your primary job, such as running a consultancy or business on the side. It can also be completely unrelated work, such as bartending on weekends or working in a retail store in the evenings.

Many companies have policies that restrict moonlighting if it violates confidentiality agreements, creates a conflict of interest, or interferes with an employee's ability to perform his or her job well. No company wants employees to use company resources or facilities for their own benefit. Federal and state agencies may impose a cap on the percentage of income that can be earned from moonlighting. Before taking on a second job, confirm that it does not violate the employment contract you signed with your primary employer. Do not conduct your private business, such as setting up appointments to show real estate properties or maintaining a private client's Web site, on company time or using company computers and telephones. If you must deal with an occasional emergency or phone call while at your regular job, discuss your situation with your boss and work out an arrangement that is satisfactory to both of you.

Ideally, your second job will either complement your primary employment and give you a chance to network and gain additional experience, or it will provide a refreshing, enjoyable contrast. There is a reason for the 40-hour work week. The extra income from a second job is important, but not at the expense of your health and the happiness of your family.

Freelancing is doing one-time projects or consultations for a fee. It is not steady employment like a second job, but it provides opportunities to use your talents or professional skills to earn extra income. Freelancing might involve creating a Web site for a small business, photographing a family reunion, setting up a home computer network for a neighbor, writing a magazine article, or preparing someone's taxes.

Moonlighting and freelancing broaden your network of contacts and add to your work experience. You may be able to experiment with a new type of career or start a business of your own without losing the security of your primary employment.

How to Get Started

Part-time and freelance job opportunities are typically posted in local classified ads, or online on Web sites like **Craigslist.org** and **Sologig.com**. You may also hear about them through word of mouth. Post your own classified ads offering your services, and tell everyone you know what you are doing. If you want to be a freelancer, create a Web site advertising what you do, and print some business cards or brochures that can be left in places where potential clients will see them. Put them on community bulletin boards in local schools, supermarkets, and churches. Place inexpensive ads in local newsletters.

Things to Keep in Mind

Document Your Work

Business is business. Before undertaking a freelance project, come to a clear understanding with your client. Write all your expectations, including the work to be done and the amount and timing of payments, on paper, and have your client sign it. Keep records of the time spent and the work done. If problems arise or you begin to deviate from the original agreement, discuss it with your client and re-negotiate your expectations. Provide your client with invoices and receipts for all payments.

Savvy Student Tip:

Some freelance projects take longer or require more work than originally expected. Limit the damage by re-negotiating your arrangement with your client. If you lose money on a project, or do not earn enough to justify the time you spent, take it as a lesson learned and develop methods of creating proposals and documenting work to prevent the same problem from happening in the future. As you gain experience, you will know how to invoice accurately for the work you do.

Liability

Protect yourself from harm by being aware of the potential liability associated with the work you do. Web site content might inadvertently violate a copyright. While clearing tree branches, you could damage a client's roof or injure yourself. A guest could have an allergic reaction to the nuts you put on a birthday cake. You cannot protect yourself from every possibility, but you can prevent common mishaps by taking common-sense precautions. Always make your safety and the safety of your clients your first priority. If you become active in a business that involves risk, consider taking steps to protect yourself, such as incorporating your business, buying insurance, and using waivers and disclaimers. Consult a lawyer or a trade association to learn about the legal options for your type of business.

Taxes and Expenses

Keep accurate records of the money you earn from your activities and any expenses you incur. File away receipts and invoices. If clients list your services as a business expense on their tax returns, you should report your earnings as business income on your tax return. Under current tax laws, a business client who pays you more than $600 in a year must file an IRS Form 1099 (Miscellaneous Income) and send you a copy.

If you report business income on your tax return, you are entitled to deductions for business-related expenses, including the purchase of inventory and supplies, equipment and machinery, mileage for the use of your car, and the use of part of your home as an office. This can be especially helpful if you have had to make an initial investment in equipment or software. You must be able to document your expenses with receipts, invoices, and corroborating evidence. Equipment such as a laptop computer does not qualify unless it is used almost 100 percent for the business. Most tax preparation software will walk you step-by-step through the process of itemizing your business expenses.

Even if you earn income by performing occasional services for individuals on a personal basis, you may want to report it and itemize your business expenses on your tax return.

Income Streams

An "income stream" is an ongoing source of income. Your primary and most reliable income stream is your job, but you can establish other small business ventures that have the potential to bring in income from time to time and may even develop into a future career. Ideally, you will be able to establish one or more "passive income streams" in which some initial effort sets up a business that continues to bring in income almost by itself. Income streams are as diverse and unique as the people who create them. Initially, look for a business that requires little or no financial investment to get started. The best type of business is one with which you are already familiar and which fits well with the resources we discussed above: your skills, interests, family and friends, and your location. If social relationships are your strength, look for a product that you can sell in your community. If you are a web designer or a blogger, use your online network to promote a business.

Multi-Level Marketing

You may cringe when you hear the term "multi-level marketing," but it exists because it succeeds for many people. Companies create a specialized, often high-end product line and provide marketing materials and sales support to thousands of individuals who sell the products directly to their personal contacts. Members who recruit new sales representatives are typically rewarded with a bonus or a small commission on their sales, and the sales of the people who are in turn recruited by the new reps. Sales representatives hold "parties," or workshops, at which they demonstrate the products and engage potential customers, and create a network of support and training for new recruits. Avon, Mary Kay, Tupperware, and The Pampered Chef® are among the most famous companies, but hundreds of products are sold in this way, including children's books, candles, clothing, educational toys, jewelry, scrapbooking materials, health foods, vitamins, cleaning supplies, and kitchenware.

The secret is to sell a product that you enjoy using yourself and about which you are enthusiastic. If you enter the network when a product is relatively new in your community, you can establish a large "downline" of new recruits. After making an initial effort for several years, you can retire and still continue to receive a percentage of your recruits' sales. Look for companies that provide generous sales support and customer service. Have a clear understanding of a company's compensation policies before becoming involved, and be wary of companies that require you to purchase a large inventory or "starter kit."

Affiliate Programs

If you have a Web site, you can sign up for affiliate programs with retailers selling products related to your interests. For example, you can sell books and music from **Amazon.com** by placing a link on your site. For every sale resulting from the link on your site, you will receive a commission. Many retailers offer affiliate programs. Some also offer "turnkey sites," complete Web sites that you can register under your name and operate as online stores. You are responsible for marketing your site to generate sales. While you should not rely on such sites for a regular income, they can supplement your budget from time to time.

You can set up a more elaborate online store for goods that a company will "drop ship" directly from its warehouse to the customer. You do the advertising and marketing, and the company takes care of customer service. Look for affiliate programs with companies that you are already familiar with. As with any business, shop around before committing yourself. Be wary of any company that charges up-front fees. Compare the prices of items on other online stores to see whether the "wholesale" prices of a drop-ship company are really competitive.

Savvy Student Tip:

Watch out for scams. There is no mysterious formula for making money. Countless Internet ads promise a business that will bring in a huge income with just a few hours of work. Stay away from business opportunities that do not explain clearly how money is made, do not give a business address or contact information, or contain unprofessional wording. Research the company and check references. Look for online reviews of the business opportunity. A legitimate business will be able to give you ample information and will provide customer service and technical support.

Selling Things

A few hundred dollars applied today to the principal of your loan balance goes a long way toward saving you money in the long run. Now may be a good time to sell your childhood stamp collection, your broken gold and silver jewelry, or an antique piece of furniture that you no longer want. Look on eBay.com and online classified ads and auctions to research the prices offered by others for similar items. Take your jewelry to a local jeweler for appraisal, have valuable stamps or other collectibles appraised by a dealer or appraiser, then put them up for auction with a minimum bid that ensures you will get what you want for them. You can always lower your minimum bid later if they do not sell. It may take some time to research and discover the best way to sell your items. Remember that dealers are buying in order to make a profit by reselling the items and will not offer you the full appraised value.

On Web sites such as **Cash4Gold.com** and **DollarsforGold.com**, you can order a mailer and send in your broken gold and silver jewelry for a cash payment. These companies buy by weight and melt the jewelry down; a jeweler might pay more for a piece that is intact and can be cleaned and resold.

If you collect something as a hobby and are knowledgeable about it, you may be able to develop a small business buying and selling online. Search auction sites and classified ads, and consider setting up a simple online store with Yahoo! Small Business (**http:// smallbusiness.yahoo.com**) or QuickShoppingCart® at **GoDaddy. com**. Account for fees, subscription charges, and shipping costs when calculating your profit.

A garage sale can net several hundred dollars if it is well-advertised or part of a community-wide garage sale. You may be able to rent a temporary spot at a local weekend flea market or antique mall to sell off clothing, shoes, and household goods that you do not need anymore. Be sure you can make enough to justify advertising or rental costs.

Sell your prom dresses and evening wear, business outfits, and designer jeans, tops, and shoes to consignment stores or second-hand stores. Consignment stores will not pay you until your clothing is sold; secondhand stores will appraise the clothes when you bring them in and pay for them on the spot.

Recycle your books, textbooks, CDs, and DVDs on sites like **Alibris.com**, **Amazon.com**, **textbooks.com**, and **textbookwheel. com**. Some sites charge a sign-up fee, and will drop you if you fail to ship your books promptly when they are sold.

CHAPTER 17

Your Other Debt

Since 1998, Nellie Mae, a Sallie Mae student loan company, has conducted six studies of credit card usage among college students. According to its fall 2006 study, 92 percent of graduate students had credit cards in 2006, with the average outstanding balance being $8,612. Of those graduate students, 15 percent had balances of more than $15,000, and 94 percent of them reported using credit cards to pay for some of their education expenses. In a 2004 study, Nellie Mae reported that 76 percent of undergraduates had credit cards, and that more than half of them had obtained their first card at the age of 18. Students in their final year at school carried an average of $2,864 in credit card debt. Based on these statistics, you likely graduated with at least some credit card debt, in addition to your student loan obligations.

Just like student loan debt, credit card debt must be wisely managed and paid off as quickly as possible. The burden of monthly credit card payments inhibits your ability to keep up with your student loan payments. Too many open credit card accounts, too much debt in proportion to your monthly income, and late or missed credit card payments have a damaging effect on your credit report and may prevent you from obtaining an auto loan or good rates on automobile insurance.

Good Debt and Bad Debt

Not all debt is bad. Large businesses use debt every day to expand production, build facilities, and conduct research that will ultimately result in increased profits. "Good debt" is debt that enables you to increase your income and is managed in a way that improves your credit rating and benefits your future financial status. An affordable mortgage with a reasonable interest rate is good debt because it provides you with a place to live while giving you a stake in real estate that will hold its value over time. Student loans are considered good debt because they allow you to obtain a college degree, have low interest rates, and build a good credit history when payments are made on time. Charges on a credit card can be "good debt" if they are paid off in full each month, or if they purchase raw materials or services that instantly produce income.

"Bad debt" is debt incurred to buy items that are beyond your means, with a high interest rate that over time doubles and even triples the cost of your purchase. Bad debt takes over your life until you are working just to make your monthly payments and are unable to advance your economic circumstances or save for the future. An example of bad debt is an auto loan with a high interest rate and low monthly payments, used to purchase a new car that loses half of its value after you have driven it off the lot. The car will rapidly depreciate in value and may be worthless before you have finished paying for it. The difference between good debt and bad debt is the choices you make in deciding when and how much to spend, and the way in which you manage your payments.

Putting Credit Cards in Their Place

Credit cards are convenient for certain purposes. Having a major credit card makes it easy for you to rent a car, and credit cards can be a safety cushion during an emergency, such as an unexpected medical expense or a blown tire. A credit card can also be used to separate certain types of expenses, such as the expenses of running a small business, or the cost of travel, from your regular spending.

Savvy Student Tip:

Never put a charge on your credit card unless you have a plan for paying it back. Ideally, the balance of your credit card should be paid off in full every month. If you decide to take on new debt by charging a major expense, such as a new refrigerator, on your credit card, you should have a specific plan for paying it back. Adjust your budget so that you can pay it back as soon as possible. .

Establishing Good Credit

If you have little or no credit history, or you want to rebuild your credit after a period of difficult finances, open a credit card account, make a few purchases with it every month, and pay them back before the due date. If you do not qualify for an unsecured credit card, you can obtain a secured credit card by making a deposit with your bank. You will be given a credit limit equal to the amount of the deposit. Secured credit cards carry many of the same benefits as unsecured cards, such as protection from unauthorized use of the card, auto rental insurance, and travel emergency assistance. Pay more than the minimum payment on time every month; if possible, pay the balance off each month. After you have established a history of regular, on-time payments, you may qualify for an unsecured credit card. There tends to be an annual fee for a secured credit card. Avoid the type of secured credit card that only allows you to make purchases from their merchandise catalog.

Although opening a credit card account helps to improve your credit history, opening too many of them does not. Do not open more than two in one year.

Managing Credit Card Debt

Managing credit card debt is more complex than managing student loans. Unlike your student loan payment, which is due on the same day every month, credit cards have billing cycles, which can be as short as 28 days. If you are accustomed to arranging all your bill payments on the same day of every month, you may find that the due date for your credit card payment occurs earlier this month than it did the month before.

Credit card agreements are fraught with traps and pitfalls. A credit card payment that is even one day late incurs a hefty late payment fee and triggers a higher interest rate on the entire loan balance. Your low promotional APR (annual percentage rate) can suddenly jump to 19 percent or more. A higher interest rate means a higher minimum payment and a rapid increase in your loan balance if it is not paid off quickly.

Read the Fine Print

Credit card offers usually come with a simple, attractive letter and a small pamphlet with tiny, closely-packed print. The sales pitch in the offering letter is only part of the story. Read the disclosures on the back of the letter and the enclosed information carefully. What is the fee for balance transfers? When does the low introductory APR expire? What interest rate applies afterwards? What are the fees and penalties for late or returned payments? How much will the minimum payment be? What is the interest rate for cash withdrawals? Knowing all the facts protects you from missteps and allows you more flexibility in making money management decisions; for example, it might be worthwhile to use a cash advance from a credit card to avoid the negative consequences of being late with a loan payment.

Pay on Time and Online

You have heard horror stories about credit card payments made by check not being posted until days or weeks after they were put in the mail, or being counted as late payments because they were postmarked after noon on the due date. Avoid uncertainty by making payments well in advance of the due date. Online payments are posted according to clearly specified guidelines and sometimes post immediately. Payment dates will show up on your bank statement. Keep a record of confirmation numbers.

Paying Off Credit Card Debt

Put Your Credit Card Away

Your primary goal is to pay off your loans and credit card balances. To avoid incurring new debt, do not carry a credit card around in your wallet. Put it away in a safe place, take it out only when you intend to use it, and then put it back. Do not use credit cards to pay for incidental expenses or impulse buys.

Lower Your Interest Rates

There are two ways to lower interest rates on your credit card debt:

1. Ask your credit card company for a lower rate

2. Refinance the debt with another loan or credit card that has a lower interest rate

If your interest rate has risen because of a late payment, call the credit card company and explain that you have been a good customer and want to find a way to lower your interest rate. Based on the financial institution's current marketing policy, your credit score, and your previous payment history, the credit card company may agree to lower the APR on your account, or offer to transfer the balance to a new account with a lower rate. Ask what the balance transfer fee is before accepting. The company may also agree to waive a late payment fee. It never hurts to ask.

Transfer High APR Balances to Another Credit Card

You can transfer a credit card balance with a high APR to another credit card with a lower APR. Shop around for new cards offering a low introductory rate, move the balance to the new card, and try to pay it off before the introductory rate expires. Most companies charge either a maximum balance transfer fee or a certain percentage of the total loan balance, but this amount will still be less than the interest you would pay on the old loan.

Savvy Student Tip:

Avoid "maxing out" with a balance transfer. Even if you do not intend to make further purchases with a card after a balance transfer, avoid transferring an amount close to the maximum credit limit onto the new card. Credit bureaus look at how much of your available credit you are using. Your credit score will be higher if you use 50 percent or less of the available credit..

Consolidate with a Lower Interest Loan

Many banks offer consolidation loans that you can use to pay off high-interest credit card balances. If you own a home, you may be able to use a home equity loan to pay off high-interest balances. Both of these types of loans have a scheduled monthly payment that may be larger than the minimum payments required by credit cards. Before transferring your credit card balance to a loan, confirm that you can afford the monthly payments.

Savvy Student Tip:

Don't close old accounts when you transfer or pay off balances. The length of your credit history is another factor that impacts your credit score. Closing an old credit card account that you have held for many years may instantly shorten your credit history and lower your score. To help maintain a good credit score, hold on to old accounts and make small purchases with them every three months, then pay them off.

Create a "Debt Snowball"

A debt snowball is a strategy to pay off credit card debt. Add your credit card accounts to the chart on which you listed all your student loans. Next to each credit card, put the amount you owe, the minimum monthly payment, and the number of months it will take to pay off the loan. You can use a calculator such as the one on **Bankrate.com**. Now, number the credit card accounts in the order you would like to pay them off. Logically, you should pay off the one with the highest interest rate first, but some experts recommend giving first priority to the smallest balance, because the satisfaction of paying it off quickly will help to motivate you.

Total up the minimum monthly payments, and set aside a slightly larger amount in your monthly budget to pay off debt. Each month, apply the slightly larger amount to credit card #1 until it is paid off. Then, begin adding the total amount you used to pay for credit card #1 to the payment for credit card #2 until it is paid off, and so on. The **Interest.com** Web site has a calculator that will show you how many months it will take to pay off all your debts, and how much you can save in interest payments by adding a few extra dollars to your payment budget.

Living with Debt

Even when you are concentrating on repaying your student loans and paying off credit card balances as quickly as possible, debt should not dominate your life or prevent you from moving forward with your personal and career goals. You may be willing to endure economic hardship while you work toward a short-term goal such as a post-graduate degree, or until you can find a good job that provides an adequate income, but placing too many restraints on yourself will lead to frustration and despair. You did not study and work hard for four or five years in school to develop your skills and your intellectual knowledge, only to graduate and live a life of deprivation and constraint. The goal is to establish a system of money management that regularly meets your monthly debt obligations, takes care of your basic needs, and allows you some freedom to enjoy the present and work toward future goals.

Striking a Balance

Your debt-to-income ratio is the percentage of your gross monthly income devoted to paying your debts. Most financial professionals agree that your debt-to-income ratio should not exceed 36 percent. Multiply your gross monthly income — monthly income before taxes — by .36. That is the maximum amount that you should be paying toward rent or mortgage, auto loans, student loan debt, and credit card debt combined. If you are paying more than that, you are in danger of encountering financial hardship and should try to find a way to lower your payments. If you are paying much less than that amount, you can afford to make larger monthly payments and pay your debt off faster. U.S. News & World Report offers an online calculator, at **www.usnews.com/ usnews/biztech/tools/modebtratio.htm**.

Financial institutions typically look at your debt-to-income ratio when determining whether to approve a loan or credit offer.

Pursuing Your Goals

Personal finance education teaches the importance of saving money in a tax-protected retirement account and investing while you are young, so that your retirement savings can grow substantially over time. In the United States, less than 25 percent of companies now offer retirement pensions; instead, each individual is expected to be responsible for setting aside his or her own money for the future. This puts pressure on you to begin saving for retirement right away. The rate at which your money will grow in a year in a retirement savings account depends both on economic factors and on the type of investments you select.

According to Standard & Poors (**www.standardandpoors.com),** the average annual compounded rate of return for the S&P500 from January 1970 to December was 9.7 percent, but it fluctuated from a high of 61 percent from June 1982 to June 1983, to -39% from September 1973 to September 1974 and from November 2007 to November 2008. If you compare the amount of interest you might (or might not) earn from the first year or two of contributions to a retirement savings plan to the interest you are paying on your high-APR credit cards, it makes sense to apply that money to your loan balances for the first few years instead. After your credit card debt is reduced, you can start saving for retirement.

Many companies that administer 401(k) plans match their employees' contributions up to a certain percentage of their salaries. This is free money. If your employer offers 401(k) matching, factor that amount into the gains from your 401(k) plan when comparing them to interest paid on your debt.

Getting Help

There is a difference between building up a debt because you use a credit card occasionally for emergencies or when you run out of money at the end of the month and continually spending money you do not have on impulse shopping. If your life seems to be in constant financial turmoil, you may have serious emotional problems that prevent you from managing money successfully. A quiz and checklist on the Debtors Anonymous Web site, at **www.debtorsanonymous.org**, can help you determine whether you are a compulsive debtor. A self-supporting, non-profit association, it offers peer support and advice for overcoming the tendency to incur ongoing credit card debt.

If you feel overwhelmed and unable to implement a financial management plan by yourself, consult a non-profit credit counseling agency. A credit counseling agency assesses your financial situation, reviews and revises your budget, helps you set goals and work out a plan to pay off your debts, provides financial education, and, in some cases, negotiates lower payments with your creditors. Working with a credit counseling agency will not harm your credit rating and may even improve your score. Look for a counseling agency through the National Foundation for Credit Counseling **(http://www.nfcc.org**, 800-388-2227) or the Association of Independent Consumer Credit Counseling Agencies **(http://www.aiccca.org**, 866-703-8787). There are many legitimate non-profit credit counseling agencies that charge reasonable fees and are staffed with licensed counselors, but there are also agencies that are primarily concerned with making money at your expense and may misrepresent themselves. Avoid agencies that advertise on the radio or TV. Before committing yourself, ask to see the company's IRS Approval of Nonprofit Status letter and the contract you will be expected to sign.

Savvy Student Tip:

Do not confuse credit counseling agencies with debt settlement firms. Debt settlement firms are businesses that charge fees for negotiating lower payments and debt settlements with creditors. You can do this kind of negotiation yourself. Debt settlement firms typically ask you to make payments to them instead of to your creditors and may cause you to miss payments and incur late fees..

Some churches, religious organizations, and service clubs offer free debt counseling and financial education.

CHAPTER 18

When Things Go Wrong

What Could Go Wrong?

Any number of circumstances can cause you to miss student loan payments, become delinquent, and eventually go into default. You may be unaware of when the loan payments first become due, or lose track of multiple loans. If the lender does not have your current address or e-mail contact information, you may not receive notice that a payment is overdue. Maybe you have moved or are away from home for a few months for seasonal employment. Your family might not understand the importance of the letters that are sent to you and neglect to forward them. If lenders or collection services phone and are told that you are not at home, they will not explain your situation to a family member or friend. You may become unable to make your regular loan payments because of illness or the sudden loss of a job, or because of some large, unexpected expense. You may feel frustrated and angry about the size of your loan payments, and deliberately ignore the notices and calls that start to arrive when you become delinquent. Your life may be disrupted because of a natural disaster, or you may be called to serve as a firefighter or medical technician in a national emergency and be unable to contact your bank or your lender for several weeks.

Earlier chapters have explained several things you can do to avoid default, such as keeping informed, setting up automated payments, contacting your lender and requesting forbearance when you cannot make payments, and adjusting the amount of your payment to match your income. What if your loans are already delinquent or in default? Default has harmful, lasting consequences, and you should immediately take steps to rectify the situation, rehabilitate your loans, and put yourself back on the track to financial stability.

Bankruptcy and Default

Student Loans are Forever

Student loans cannot be discharged through bankruptcy. Before 1976, student loans could be canceled by declaring personal bankruptcy. The US Bankruptcy Code (11 USC 101 et seq), introduced in 1978, excluded federally insured loans or private loans made by a "nonprofit institution of higher education" from the types of debt that could be discharged by bankruptcy. Gradually, the laws were modified to exclude all private education loans from discharge through bankruptcy.

Section 220 of the Bankruptcy Abuse Prevention and Consumer Protection Act of 2005 (BAPCPA), P.L. 109-8, effective October 17, 2005, reads:

"523(a) Exceptions to discharge

(8) unless excepting such debt from discharge under this paragraph would impose an undue hardship on the debtor and the debtor's dependents, for --

> i. an educational benefit overpayment or loan made, insured, or guaranteed by a governmental unit, or made under any program funded in whole or in part by a governmental unit or nonprofit institution; or

> ii. an obligation to repay funds received as an educational benefit, scholarship, or stipend; or

>> A. any other educational loan that is a qualified education loan, as defined in section 221(d)(1) of the Internal Revenue Code of 1986, incurred by a debtor who is an individual;"

A qualifying education loan is a loan made specifically to pay the higher education expenses of a student who is either the borrower or the spouse or dependent of the borrower and is enrolled at least half-time at a school that qualifies to participate in Title IV programs. Other types of loans, such as credit card debt or home equity loans, are dischargeable through bankruptcy, even if they were used to pay for higher education expenses.

The only way to discharge a student loan through bankruptcy is to prove in court that repaying the loan would cause you substantial and undue hardship. It is rare for a judge to approve the cancellation of a student loan. If you are absolutely unable to repay a student loan because, for example, you have become disabled or your income is extremely low, try other options, such as a disability discharge or an income-based repayment plan.

Savvy Student Tip:

Consumer advocates are concerned that the provisions excluding private student loans from bankruptcy discharge under the Bankruptcy Abuse Prevention and Consumer Protection Act of 2005 may trap student borrowers in a hopeless cycle of debt. Private student loans are not regulated by the restrictions governing federally-insured loans. Interest rates on private loans are not fixed or capped; they are variable and based on the credit-worthiness of the borrower. Borrowers of private student loans are in danger of being saddled with a lifelong obligation to pay off their debts at extremely high interest rates.

Eligibility for Financial Aid

Old federal student loans that were discharged in bankruptcy proceedings will not affect your eligibility for federal student aid if you decide to return to school. Changes introduced by the Bankruptcy Reform Act of 1994 (P.L. 103-394, enacted October 22, 1994) no longer require borrowers who had FFEL loans previously discharged in bankruptcy to reinstate those loans before they can receive additional federal student aid. You will not be eligible for federal financial aid if you have any current student loans in default or delinquency. Contact your lender or loan servicer to set up a repayment plan and restore your eligibility for federal financial aid.

Parents applying for a PLUS loan may be turned down if they have filed for bankruptcy within the past five years. They may still qualify for a PLUS loan if they can find a credit-worthy co-signer.

A previous bankruptcy affects a borrower's eligibility for private student loans. Many private loan programs require a credit-worthy cosigner if the borrower has declared bankruptcy within the past seven to ten years. There may be extenuating circumstances, such as a bankruptcy filed because of an extreme medical emergency or a natural disaster. A parent's bankruptcy does not affect the student's eligibility for private student loans. If you have declared bankruptcy in the past, and are now applying for student loans, discuss your situation with a financial aid advisor at your school.

Avoiding Default by Consolidating Your Loans

Your federal student loan does not go into default until after you have missed nine months of monthly payments — eleven months for loans with payments scheduled less frequently. If you include your six-month grace period — nine months for Perkins loans — you have a relatively long time after graduation before your delinquent loans go into default. You can avoid default by consolidating the delinquent loan and other federal loans into a new federal consolidation loan with a repayment plan appropriate for your income.

Private loans are considered to be in default after 120 days of non-payment. You can avoid default on a delinquent loan by seeking a private consolidation loan, which means replacing one private loan with another. Private student lenders cannot withhold your income tax refunds or garnish your Social Security payments if you default on a private loan, but they can sue for wage garnishment.

Borrowers can consolidate most defaulted federal education loans in a Direct Consolidation Loan by making satisfactory arrangements for repayment with the current loan holders or by applying for a Direct Loan Income Contingent Repayment Plan.

To receive an FFEL Consolidation Loan, you must arrange for repayment with the holder of your defaulted loan and make three voluntary, on-time, full monthly payments. After an FFEL student loan is placed in default, the guaranty agency that administers the FFEL program for your state pays the loan holder the full amount of the loan. You must then contact the agency servicing your loan to find out about your repayment options. If you do not know which guaranty agency holds your defaulted loan, call the Federal Student Aid Information Center, at 1-800-4-FED-AID (1-800-433-3243).

Savvy Student Tip:

You can consolidate FFEL loans into a Direct consolidation loan without having defaulted. Sections 7015(c) and 7015(d) of Public Law 109-234, the Emergency Supplemental Appropriations Act for Defense, the Global War on Terror, and Hurricane Recovery, June 15, 2006, repealed the restriction that FFEL loans must be in default before they can be consolidated in a Direct consolidation loan.

If your student loan has gone into default, and your lender has turned it over to a collection agency, you are responsible for paying "reasonable collection costs," in addition to the amount of the original loan and late fees. Under government guidelines, these collections costs may equal 25 to 40 percent of the outstanding loan balance and principal. When you consolidate a defaulted federal student loan, collection fees of up to 18.5 percent can be included in the consolidation loan. Some collection agencies will agree to waive additional collection costs if you consolidate. If the collection agency does not agree to waive the remainder of its fees, you will be responsible for paying them separately from the loan.

Once your federal loan has been consolidated, you will again be eligible for other federal funds, including FHA loans, VA loans, and Title IV student financial aid funds.

Rehabilitating Your Loan

The Department of Education offers guidelines for returning your defaulted federal student loans to in-payment status — rehabilitation. The first step is to contact your lender or the guaranty agency holding your loan and tell them that you wish to re-enter payment on your defaulted loan. The loan service will determine a "reasonable and affordable payment" based on your disposable monthly income and financial situation. You must then make nine voluntary full payments of the agreed amount within 20 days of their monthly due dates over a ten-month period to the U.S. Department of Education. Funds secured from you during that period through wage garnishment or litigation do not count as voluntary payments. For Perkins loans with longer payment intervals, you must make nine consecutive voluntary payments. Once these payments have been made, a Direct Loan will be returned to the Direct Loan Servicing Center, and an FFEL loan may be purchased by an eligible lender. Perkins loans will continue to be serviced by the Department of Education.

You will become eligible for additional federal financial aid, such as Pell Grants, subsidized and unsubsidized Stafford Loans, and Perkins Loans after you have made six voluntary full payments within fifteen days of the due date.

Once you have completed the rehabilitation process, your loans will no longer be considered in default, and the default status reported by your lender to the national credit bureaus will be eliminated. Your wages and income tax refunds will no longer be subject to garnishment. Deferment, forbearance, and other benefits that were associated with your loans before they went into default will be restored. You will again become eligible for federal student loans and financial aid. You will also become eligible for other federal programs, such as VA and HUD mortgages.

For more information on rehabilitating your loans, see FSA Collections on the Federal Student Aid Web site, at **www.ed.gov/offices/OSFAP/DCS/repaying.html**.

Savvy Student Tip:

Adjust your payment plan after rehabilitation. Once your student loan has been rehabilitated, it will return to the ten-year Standard Repayment Plan, and the monthly payments will be higher than the "reasonable and affordable" payments you made during the rehabilitation period. Contact your lender to switch to an income-sensitive or extended repayment plan to keep your payments manageable.

A+

SAVVY STUDENT

When the Bill Collectors Call

After you miss a second payment on a government loan, the Department of Education requires the lender to notify the guarantor that you are delinquent and in danger of defaulting on the loan. The guarantor then employs collection specialists to send you warning letters and contact you by phone until satisfactory arrangements are made to pay the loan. These efforts are known as "due diligence" and are required by the Department of Education, and neither the lender nor the guarantor can deviate from them. If you fail to respond to these notices, your loan will go into default.

You will never experience a call from a bill collector if you have followed the steps outlined earlier in this book. If your student loan is in delinquency or default, and a bill collector calls you, remember that he or she is not your personal enemy, just an employee hired to help you make arrangements to pay off your loan. Your loan Promissory Note includes a clause granting permission for the lender's agents to contact you.

If you are simply behind on a payment and can find enough money, the easiest thing to do is to make the payment. If your circumstances are more complicated, or you are unable to make the payment, explain this to the bill collector and ask for help. The collector should then ask you some questions to see whether you qualify for any type of deferment. The next option is forbearance. You will be asked when you expect to be able to begin repaying your loan again. Some lenders allow forbearance in small increments; others require that you take six or twelve months of forbearance. After you have reached an oral agreement over the phone, most lenders will send you a formal written notice.

While you are on the phone, be sure to get all the contact information for your lender.

Once you have entered forbearance, immediately make plans for paying off the loan in the future, using all the options explained in this book. Remember that interest accrues during forbearance and will be added to your loan principal, and make whatever payments you can during the period of forbearance. Keep a record of the date forbearance ends, and the date when your first payment after forbearance will be due.

Savvy Student Tip:

*The Department of Education does not have the status of a debt collection agency, but professional debt collectors are restricted by the federal Fair Debt Collection Practices Act (**www.ftc.gov/bcp/edu/pubs/ consumer/credit/cre27.pdf**), administered by the Federal Trade Commission. A debt collector cannot call you before 8 a.m., after 9 p.m., or at work without your permission; he or she also cannot threaten or harass you or use deceptive practices. Some states have additional regulations regarding debt collectors. For more information, see the Federal Trade Commission Web site, at **www.ftc.gov/bcp/edu/pubs/ consumer/credit/cre18.shtm**, or the Privacy Rights Clearinghouse Web site, at **www.privacyrights.org/fs/fs27-debtcoll.htm**.*

Where to Go for Help

If you need to make payment arrangements, are in danger of default, believe that a payment has not been accurately recorded, or have a question about your loan, contact your lender or loan servicer. In Chapter 9, you can find help in locating your lender. The person who first answers the phone may not be knowledgeable enough to give an answer about a complicated situation; explain your situation fully, and enlist his or her help in finding the right person to speak to.

While you are in school, or if you plan to return to school, you can get counseling and assistance from the school's financial aid department.

The office of the Federal Student Aid Ombudsman was created by the Department of Education in 1998 to resolve disputes concerning student loans. The Ombudsman will informally investigate complaints from a neutral, independent viewpoint and recommend solutions. If it finds a complaint to be justified, it will contact other offices within the U.S. Department of Education, your private lender, your loan guaranty agency, and the servicing or collection agency on your behalf. The Ombudsman Web site, at (**http://ombudsman.ed.gov/**) has numerous resources that can answer your questions and help you resolve your own problems.

The National Consumer Law Center's Student Borrower Assistance Program, at **www.studentloanborrowerassistance.org**, offers step-by-step guidance for solving student loan problems, and answers to a wide array of questions.

CHAPTER 19

The Final Option: Loan Discharge

There are several circumstances under which federal loan obligations will be completely discharged. Your case must meet specific requirements, and you will be required to submit documentation to support your application. The approval process can take several months, and you may need to submit documents more than once if there is even a minor error or if information is missing. Forms, instructions, and detailed rules are posted on the Department of Education Web site, at **www.ed.gov/offices/OSFAP/DCS/forms.html**, or can be mailed to you if you call 1-800-4-FED-AID (1-800-433-3243).

If you qualify for federal student loan discharge, you must apply for it. Federal Perkins Loan borrowers must apply to the school that made the loan or to the loan servicer designated by the school. Borrowers of Direct Stafford and PLUS loans must contact the Direct Loan Servicing Center. FFEL Stafford and PLUS loan borrowers should contact the lender or the agency holding the loan. For most discharges, the holder of your loan makes the final decision on whether to discharge the loan; you cannot appeal the decision to the U.S. Department of Education.

Private lenders may offer discharges under certain circumstances, but they are not required to. Read each private loan's promissory note to find out more. Borrowers of private loans or of federal loans not eligible for the discharges may be able to raise some of these issues as defenses to a collection action if a lender takes them to court to enforce payment.

Death

The death of a borrower discharges his or her federal student loan obligations, and the obligation of a parent borrower on a Parent PLUS loan. An original or certified copy of the death certificate — with a raised seal — must be submitted to the school for a Federal Perkins Loan or to the holder of the loan for an FFEL or Direct Stafford Loan. The death of a parent who took out a PLUS loan is also grounds for the "death discharge." If both parents took out the loan, the death of only one of the two obligated parents does not cancel a PLUS loan.

There is no administrative discharge for private student loans when the borrower dies. Private loan debts will be handled the same way as other debts, and will be part of the borrower's estate. The estate settlement process — also called probate — varies by state. More information can be found in the promissory note. Lenders must also be notified of the death of a cosigner.

When notifying a lender about the death of the primary borrower, cosigner, or student on an account, you may be asked to provide information such as date of death; city, county, and state where the death occurred; name and address of the hospital or funeral home; executor or best person to contact; and mother's maiden name and father's name. Additional documents may be required.

Permanent Disability

You can receive a permanent disability discharge from an FFEL, Direct, or Perkins loan if a physician of medicine or osteopathy who is licensed to practice in the U.S. certifies that you are unable to work and earn an income because of an illness or injury that is expected to continue indefinitely or result in death. The U.S. Department of Education has its own standards for determining disability, and they are more restrictive than the standards used to determine eligibility for Social Security or other government disability benefits. To be eligible, you must meet the definition of total and permanent disability provided in Section 5 of the Loan Discharge Application: Total and Permanent Disability (**www.ed.gov/offices/OSFAP/DCS/forms.html**). A new provision in the Higher Education Opportunity Act states that borrowers who have been determined by the Secretary of Veterans Affairs to be unemployable due to a service-connected condition and who provide documentation of this determination are eligible for the student loan discharge and will not be required to provide additional documentation.

Parents with PLUS loans may apply for discharge based on their own disabilities, not those of their children. Consolidation loans may be canceled only if the borrower qualifies for a disability discharge for all the loans that are included in the Consolidation Loan.

The first step is to fill out the Loan Discharge Application: Total and Permanent Disability (**http://www.ed.gov/offices/OSFAP/DCS/forms/disable.pdf**) and return it to your loan holder. Missing information can delay or sidetrack the application process, so follow the instructions carefully. Have the doctor give a detailed report of your condition and submit as much information as possible about your disability. Make sure all supporting documentation is submitted together with the application. Tell your doctor that he or she may receive follow-up letters and requests from the loan holder and Department of Education, and that some of these require an immediate response. Many applications are held up because doctors are not able to respond to repeated requests for additional information.

Before July 1, 2008, doctors were required to certify the date that your disability began, and any federal student loans taken out after the onset of the disability were not eligible for discharge. Applications submitted before July 1, 2008 are subject to this rule. If you had a medical condition when you took out the student loan that did not deteriorate into a total and permanent disability until later, you should still be eligible for discharge. New rules in effect as of July 1, 2008 no longer require doctors to certify the date that your disability began, only to certify that you are totally and permanently disabled as of the date of application for discharge. If you received a disbursement of a federal loan after the date the doctor signed the form, you can still qualify for the discharge, as long as you return the funds to the loan holder within 120 days of the disbursement date.

The loan holder, such as a guaranty agency, will review your application and make a preliminary determination. If the application is accepted, it will be sent to the Department of Education for further review. You should receive a letter from your loan holder explaining this process.

If the Department agrees with the preliminary decision of the loan holder, you will be placed in a three-year conditional discharge period. During this period, the Department of Education will continue to require updates from your doctor concerning your medical condition and will monitor your IRS records to see whether you are making an income. The three-year period begins on the date the doctor signed the completed application form. You will get a final discharge at the end of this period, as long as you do not take out any new federal student loans during the three years. You cannot be working at the time the doctor signs the form, but you are allowed to try to work during the conditional period, as long as you do not have earnings from work that are more than 100 percent of the poverty line for a family of two. If you earn more than this amount, the Department assumes you are not permanently disabled.

According to the Department of Education, the approval process can take as long as a year to complete. Once you submit a completed application, collection efforts should stop until a decision is made, and interest should not accrue during this period. If your application is approved, you will get a notice of final discharge. A final discharge means that the loan is canceled and all loan payments, whether voluntary or involuntary, received after the doctor signed the form should be returned. If your application is denied, you will receive a notice giving a vague explanation for the denial, such as "medical review failure." Contact the loan holder or Department of Education Disability Unit and ask for the specific reasons for the denial. You may apply again if you were denied because of some minor problem, such as incomplete documentation, or if your condition has worsened. You may also appeal denials to federal court.

9/11 Victims

From time to time, Congress approves student loan cancellation for borrowers who have experienced a specific hardship. In 2007, student loan cancellation was approved for certain victims of the 9/11 terrorist attacks. Borrowers of Perkins, FFEL, and Direct loans can have their loans discharged if they were public servants such as police officers, firefighters, other safety or rescue personnel, or members of the Armed Forces who died or became permanently and totally disabled due to injuries suffered in the September 11 attacks. Their spouses are also eligible for loan forgiveness. Individuals who died or became permanently and totally disabled due to injuries suffered in the September 11 attacks, their spouses, and parents may be able to get discharges. Parents may only discharge PLUS loans incurred on behalf of children who were victims of the attacks.

The discharge applies to loan amounts owed as of September 11, 2001 and to consolidation loans taken out to pay off loans owed as of September 11, 2001. You must still owe something on the loan when you apply, and you cannot get a refund of payments that you already made. Applicants for this discharge will have to provide documentation of the individual's presence at one of the sites of the terrorist attacks on September 11, 2001; the individual's status as an eligible public servant for those applying under this category; and documentation that the individual's death or permanent and total disability was a direct result of the attacks.

School-Related Cancellations

Several student loan cancellation programs intended to help borrowers who are victims of fraud or school closures were enacted in response to tragic abuses, mainly in the proprietary school sector, during the late 1980s and early1990s. In May 2005, Department of Education Inspector General John P. Higgins testified that the student financial assistance program remains vulnerable and that the Department of Education's institutional assessment model is an ineffective tool for identifying "at risk" institutions. The requirements for these cancellations are restrictive and may exclude some people who feel they are entitled to a loan discharge, particularly if there was an affiliation between the school and the lender.

If your cancellation is granted, you are no longer obligated to repay the loan or any charges or costs associated with the loan. You also have the right to be reimbursed for all amounts paid on the loan, whether those payments were voluntary or involuntary. You are no longer in default on these loans, and the loan holder must report this to the credit bureaus and help clean up your credit history. If the discharge is denied, you may appeal to federal court.

To avoid making payments on a loan during the approval process, you can request forbearance; interest will still accrue on the loan. If you want to return to school before a decision on the discharge has been made, consider repayment, loan rehabilitation, and consolidation options so that you can restore your eligibility for financial aid.

School Closure

You cannot get your student loans canceled simply because you were dissatisfied with a school or could not get a job with your degree. If there is a genuine legal problem with the school you attended, such as the school closing its doors before your course of study was complete, you can apply for a federal loan discharge.

If your school closes while you are enrolled, and you can not complete your program because of the closure, any U.S. Department of Education loan obtained to pay your cost of attendance at that school can be discharged. If you were on an approved leave of absence when the school closed, you are considered to have been enrolled at the school. If your school closed within 90 days after you withdrew, you are also considered eligible for the discharge. Your loan cannot be cancelled if personal circumstances caused you to withdraw more than 90 days before the school closed — there are some cases in which the Department of Education extends the 90-day period. You are also not eligible for the discharge if you transferred your course credits to another school and are completing an equivalent educational program there, or if you have completed all the course work but have not received a diploma or certificate. The Federal Student Aid (FSA) Web site maintains a database of school closings, at **http://wdcrobcolp01.ed.gov/CFAPPS/FSA/closedschool/searchpage.cfm**, that includes information on the dates when schools officially closed. If you have evidence, such as dated newspaper articles or declarations from students and staff that these dates are incorrect, you can petition the Department of Education. The holder of your loan will send you a loan discharge application when a school closes. If you do not receive an application, contact your loan holder. You may need to obtain copies of your school records to substantiate your claims; contact the state licensing agency in the state in which the school was located to ask whether the state made arrangements to store the records.

If you have a consolidation loan that includes loans eligible for cancellation under this provision, you can apply for discharge of only those loans.

If you are applying for aid at a new school, the school's financial aid office can check the Financial Aid History information included either on the Student Aid Report you received or in the electronic record the school receives. If you are transferring in the middle of the year, your new school must check your information in the National Student Loan Data System (NSLDS).

False Certification

Ability to Benefit

False certification discharges apply only to FFEL and Direct Stafford Loans. A Stafford Loan can be discharged if the school admitted you based on your ability to benefit (ATB) from the training, but you were not properly tested to measure that ability, or you failed the test. If you enter a school without a GED or high-school diploma, the school administers an ATB exam to determine whether you have the necessary skills to benefit from the course of study. If the exam was administered incorrectly, or was not approved by the Department of Education, you may qualify for a loan discharge.

You might also be eligible for this type of discharge if you did not meet the physical or legal requirements of your state to enroll in the program or to work in the career for which you were training, regardless of whether you had a high-school diploma or General Education Development (GED) certificate. Under most circumstances, a high-school diploma or GED is considered sufficient to establish your ability to benefit from further training after high school. You may not be eligible for a discharge if you received a GED before you completed your program of study at the college or career school, or you completed a developmental or remedial program at the school.

Your application should be supported by as much documentation as possible. In some cases, a state or federal agency may have issued a report about problems with the school's ATB exams. You can ask for The Department of Education's files on a school through a Freedom of Information Act (FOIA) request. Both the Department of Education's Office of Hearings and Appeals and Office of Inspector General have reports online, which sometimes include helpful information about problems at particular schools. There is no deadline for submitting your application. Direct Loan borrowers must apply to the Department of Education, and FFEL borrowers should apply to the lender or agency holding the loan. If this is a guaranty agency, the agency is supposed to respond within 90 days.

Disqualifying Status

You are eligible for this discharge if, at the time of enrollment, you would not have been able to meet the state requirements for employment in the occupation for which you were being trained. The reasons for failure to meet the minimum requirements could be a physical or mental condition, age, criminal record, or any other reason accepted by the Department of Education. For example, you might be unqualified to work as a teacher because you have a criminal record. If a school was aware of your criminal record but still accepted you into the teacher training program, you may be able to get your student loan cancelled. If a school certifies you because you did not disclose this information on your admissions application, you are not likely to obtain a loan cancellation.

Unauthorized Signature

If someone forged your signature on your FFEL or Direct Loan promissory note or authorization for electronic fund transfer, you can apply for a loan discharge and attach five different samples of your signature to your application. At least two of the samples must be on documents that are clearly dated within a year before or after the date of the contested signature. If the loan was used to pay your school charges, whether the payment was by a credit to your account or by cash or check, you may not be eligible for this discharge.

Unpaid Refund

Students who leave school early and do not complete 60 percent of the period covered by a loan do not have to repay the full loan amount. Borrowers who never attended classes or who attended for an extremely short time should be able to get a complete cancellation of their loans. The school should return at least some of the money to the lender and make sure that it is applied to the balance of the loan. If you left school early and did not receive a refund, you may be able to apply for an unpaid refund discharge. Liability for FFEL and Direct Loans obtained after January 1, 1986 may be canceled if the school failed to pay a refund required under federal law, regardless of whether the school is open or closed.

If you never received an owed refund, you are eligible to reduce your student loan obligation by the amount that should have been refunded plus interest and related charges. If you were owed a refund for less than what you borrowed, you will only get the amount of the refund discharged, and you will still owe the rest. The amount of the unpaid refund will be calculated based on the tuition, the school's refund formula, and the percentage of the course or term that you completed. The school catalog or the written enrollment agreement should contain this information, and state licensing agencies sometimes have it as well. If the actual school refund formula is not available, the Department of Education regulations stipulate a substitute formula.

Identity Theft

A borrower who is a victim of identity theft can qualify for a student loan discharge by providing a copy of a court verdict or judgment that conclusively determines that he or she was a victim of a crime of identity theft. Since most cases of identity theft do not result in criminal convictions, this is a difficult requirement to fulfill. In addition to proof of a crime, the application must be accompanied by a letter explaining how the crime relates to the student loan, and copies of identification documents, such as a Social Security card, passport, and driver's license. You should also submit an identity theft report under the Fair Credit Reporting Act to your lender. This report must include a copy of an official report of identity theft filed with a law enforcement agency. Once you submit this identity theft report, your lender must suspend credit bureau reporting for a period of up to 120 days, while it determines whether the loan is enforceable. It is possible that the lender will find that the loan is unenforceable, even though the borrower does not qualify for a false certification identity theft discharge. In this case, the lender must report its findings to credit bureaus. The borrower should not be liable for the loan, and the lender should stop trying to collect payments.

Extreme Circumstances

You are not eligible for a loan discharge simply because personal circumstances caused you to drop out of school, you are not satisfied with the quality of your education, or you are not able to get a job in your chosen field — unless you were falsely certified, as explained on the previous page. When you take out a student loan, you are entering into a business contract that contains strong provisions for its enforcement. No matter how unjust it might seem, you are responsible for fulfilling your obligations under that contract.

If you believe that a school used deceptive practices to lure you into taking out a loan to pay for education expenses, but do not qualify for a school discharge, you may be able to seek relief from a State Tuition Recovery Fund (STRF). Many states require educational institutions, including those offering vocational programs, to pay into a fund that reimburses victims of fraudulent schools. Contact your state consumer affairs department for more information.

Federal loans offer a number of flexible repayment options, including income-based repayment plans that allow you to adjust the size of your monthly payments. These enable you to meet your debt obligations and stay out of default, even if you are saddled with a large loan balance and find you are unable to earn as much as you expected. If you are graduating with a large amount in federal student loan debt, consider taking a job that qualifies you for one of the federal loan forgiveness programs.

Private loans do not have the same discharge or loan forgiveness provisions as federal loans, or the same flexibility in repayment plans. Discuss all your repayment options with your lender. If your credit rating has improved since you first took out a private loan, or you have a creditworthy cosigner, you may be able to consolidate your private loans and get a lower interest rate and more favorable repayment terms, such as extended repayment and a lower monthly payment. If you have access to a low-interest home equity loan or line of credit, and the interest on your student loan is high, consider "refinancing" and paying off the student loan. The repayment terms for the home equity loan will be different. Public service programs like AmeriCorps will not pay off private loans, but the Peace Corps provides a $6,000 transition allowance at the end of service that could be applied to your loan. Some private employers may offer a signing bonus that you can use to pay off part of your loan balance. Student loans cannot ordinarily be discharged in bankruptcy, unless you can demonstrate to the judge that making regular loan payments will cause you and your family undue economic hardship. A judge may grant relief in the form of lower payments.

CHAPTER 20

Student Loans and Taxes

Tax Credit for Interest Paid on Student Loans

Each year, you can deduct up to $2,500 in student loan interest from your taxable income, subject to certain restrictions. The loan must have been taken out solely to pay for qualified education expenses for you, your spouse, or your dependent. The rules for this tax deduction are slightly different from those that apply to other education tax credits. For purposes of the Student Loan Interest Deduction, you can count someone as your dependent even if you are listed as a dependent on someone else's tax return or filed jointly with your spouse. A student can be considered your dependent even if his or her gross income was equal to or more than the exemption amount for the year — $3,500 for 2008. This is significant because scholarships are counted as taxable income, and many students receive more than $3,500 in annual scholarships.

Only the person legally obligated to pay the loan can claim the exemption. If you worked for a program such as AmeriCorps that paid off part of a loan on your behalf, you can claim the interest deduction as though you made the payment yourself. If your parents made some payments for you, but did not claim an exemption for you on their tax return, you can claim the deduction.

The loan cannot be from a relative or a qualified employer plan.

The loan proceeds must have been used, for qualified education expenses, within a reasonable time after the loan was disbursed. This condition is automatically met by federal loans disbursed through schools; for other types of loans, a reasonable time period is considered to be within 90 days before or after an academic period.

The interest deduction is treated as an adjustment to income and can be taken even if you do not itemize your deductions.

In 2008, the student loan interest deduction was the smaller of $2,500 or the total amount of student loan interest paid during the year. To get the maximum deduction in 2008, your Modified Adjusted Gross Income (MAGI) had to be $55,000 or less — $115,000 for married couples filing jointly. The MAGI is the Adjusted Gross Income (AGI) minus any deductions for tuition, fees, and student loan interest. If your MAGI was more than $70,000 — $145,000 for married couples filing jointly — in 2008, you did not receive any student loan interest deduction.

Qualified Education Expenses

Qualified education expenses are expanded for the student loan interest deduction to include tuition and fees; room and board; books, supplies and equipment; and other necessary expenses, such as transportation. Room and board is the allowance determined by

If your Form 1098-E does not include the loan origination fee, you can use a "reasonable" method to allocate a portion of the loan origination fee to each payment over the life of the loan, multiply that amount by the number of payments made during the year, and add it to the interest listed on the form. Next, add any outstanding capitalized interest. (Leftover capitalized interest can be added to the next year's deduction.) This is the total amount of the student loan interest deduction.

Do not count interest paid on a loan you were not legally obligated to pay, such as interest on a loan payment you made for your child who was the legal borrower; loan service fees and commissions; or interest on payments made through certain Loan Repayment Assistance Programs (LRAPs).

More information on the Student Loan Interest Deduction can be found in *IRS Publication 970, Tax Benefits for Education*, available at **www.irs.gov/publications/p970/ch04.html**.

Taxes and Loan Forgiveness

Cancelled Loans

When your federal student loan is canceled or forgiven, the amount of the cancellation must typically be reported as part of your gross income on your tax return for that year, but certain canceled loans receive tax-free treatment. To qualify, the loan must contain a provision that all or part of the debt will be canceled if you work for a certain period of time in certain professions, for any of a broad class of employers. The borrower must have received the loan to attend a qualified education institution. The lender must be one of the following:

the educational institution in their Cost of Attendance (CO
the actual amount paid to live in a school residence hall.

Interest on consolidated or collapsed student loans is eligib
the deduction, as long as the full amount of the loan was use
educational expenses. Interest on a revolving line of credit,
as a credit card, can be deducted if the card was used onl
education expenses.

In calculating your qualified education expenses, you mus
duct any amounts paid by employer-sponsored education
sistance, tax-free education savings plans, tax-free portion
scholarships and grants, U.S. Veteran's education benefits,
tax-free bonds.

Calculating the Deduction

Loan origination fees and capitalized interest can be coun
as interest in calculating the deduction. You will receive a fo
1098-E from your lender or loan servicer with a breakdown
the interest and principal paid on your loan over the year. T
allocation of interest and principal reported on Form 1098-E m
not be the same as the allocation used by the IRS for tax purpose
Capitalized interest is still treated as interest. The IRS allocate
each loan payment in this order:

1. Stated unpaid interest

2. Loan origination fee, if any

3. Capitalized interest

4. Outstanding principal

A federal, state, or local government agency.

A tax-exempt public benefit corporation that has assumed control of a state, county, or municipal hospital and whose employees are considered public employees under state law.

A qualified educational institution administering the loan on behalf of a government agency or public benefit corporation or under a program that trains students to serve in occupations with unmet needs, where the service required of the students is under the direction of a government unit or a tax-exempt organization. This government unit or tax-exempt organization under which the student is serving cannot be the lender.

A community service loan forgiveness provision allows the tax exemption for student loans that are forgiven by non-profit, tax-exempt charitable or educational institutions, for borrowers employed in community service jobs in areas of unmet need.

Student Loan Repayment Assistance

Loan repayment assistance programs (LRAPs) provide help in repaying student loans for those who work in public service occupations or in areas with unmet needs. Examples of such occupations are health care professionals in underserved areas, attorneys in legal-aid offices and prosecutor's or public defender's offices, and classroom teachers in subject areas with shortages.

Loan Repayment Assistance Programs (LRAPs) refinance original student loans with new loans that are forgiven after the borrower works for a minimum period of time in a qualifying position in public service occupations or areas with unmet needs. LRAPs are typically administered by state agencies or by educational institutions and make it possible for highly-educated professionals to work in public service. Amounts forgiven under LRAPs are tax-exempt if the LRAP meets criteria similar to those for the tax-exempt canceled loans above. The National Health Service Corps (NHSC) Loan Repayment Program, state programs under the Public Health Service Act, and law school LRAPs have been determined to be tax-exempt. Contact the administrators of an LRAP program to see whether it qualifies for tax exemption.

Tax Deduction for Mortgage Interest

If you decide to refinance your student loan debt using a home equity loan, you will be able to get a tax deduction for the mortgage interest paid on the loan every year.

CHAPTER 21

Quick Tips for Paying Off Your Student Loans Fast

- Start paying now. Start paying off your loan as soon as it is disbursed, or at least making interest payments while you are still in school. Make interest payments or partial payments even during periods of forbearance and deferment.

- Read all the loan documents, and make note of deadlines and payment dates and amounts. Know all your repayment options.

- Make an extra payment. If you budget for one loan payment every four weeks instead of every month, you will end up making 13 payments in a year instead of 12. Notify your lender that the extra payment is to be applied only to your loan principal; otherwise, it will be treated as a regular monthly payment.

- Lower your interest rate. Take advantage of all available discounts for on-time payment, electronic debit, and signing up for electronic correspondence. If you have a private high-interest loan, consolidate at a lower interest rate when your credit score has improved, or refinance with another low-interest loan.

- Take advantage of loan forgiveness programs. Pay off part of your federal loans by serving in AmeriCorps, enlisting in the military, or working in the public service or as a teacher or medical practitioner in an area of critical need. Look for jobs that offer to pay off some of your loan as an incentive.

- Make a budget and stick to it. Avoid other types of debt, such as credit card debt, by living within your means. Cut back on expenses so that you can pay more than your scheduled monthly loan payments.

- Dedicate extra income to your loan payments. Put gifts, windfalls, or income from a second job toward your student loan. You will save money by paying off your loan early, and when it is paid off, you will be free to devote your money to other purposes.

- Be proactive in managing your loans. Use forbearance or income-sensitive repayment during times of financial difficulty to avoid going into default. Make payments on time to avoid late fees.

- Build up a good credit rating by managing your debt obligations well so that you can save money by getting lower interest rates and concessions on mortgages, auto loans, and insurance premiums.

- Make paying off your debt a financial priority. Make it your goal to live debt-free and to put money aside for your future, instead of spending hundreds of extra dollars on interest. Look at your whole financial picture, not just your immediate situation, when making decisions about using money.

APPENDIX A

Creating a Repayment Plan

Step 1: Student Loan Summary

Gather all your student loan documents and fill in the chart below. When you have finished, total up the outstanding loan balance and the total monthly payments. You can print out and fill in the worksheet from FinAid.org if you prefer (**www.finaid.org/loans/studentloanchecklist.phtml**).

Student Loan Summary

School and Type of Loan	Loan #1	Loan #2	Loan #3	Loan #4	Loan #5
Loan Servicer and Contact Info					
URL, Log in and Password					
Origination Date					
End Date					
Amt of Loan					
Principal Outstanding (Date)					

Interest Out-standing (Date)					
Interest					
Interest Rate					
Status					
Entered Repay-ment					
Monthly Payment Amount					
Date Due Every Month					
Interest - Re-paymt 10 Years					
Total					

Step 2: Debt Obligations

List all your debt obligations, including mortgage, auto loans, and credit card debt on the chart below. In the first row, put the total from your student loan chart:

Debt Obligations

Company	Acct No.	Balance	APR	Minimum Monthly Payment	Months to Pay Off
Student Loans					
TOTAL					

Step 3: Income

List all your regular monthly income from all sources. If your income is irregular, list your income over a period of several months, and divide by the number of months.

Income Summary

Source	Amount
TOTAL	

Step 4: Debt-to-income Ratio

Take your total monthly debt from Step 2, and divide it by your total income from Step 3. This will give you your debt-to-income ratio.

Step 5: Adjust your Payments

If your debt-to-income ratio exceeds 21 percent, you are overextending yourself and will need to be careful. If it exceeds 36 percent, you are in financial danger and need to take action to reduce the size of your loan payments, such as switching to an extended or income-based repayment plan or asking for forbearance or deferment until you can increase your income.

Are your circumstances only temporary? Are you looking for employment, or do you expect your income to increase when you start a new job next month? If so, live frugally for the present, and revisit your debt-to-income ratio in two or three months.

Are you expecting a windfall, such as a tax refund or a resettlement allowance from the Peace Corps? Use it to pay down your student loan balance, which will lower your monthly payment, or to eliminate credit card debt or another debt obligation.

Step 6: Create a Budget

Gather your bank statements, credit card statements, and cash receipts and write down your monthly living expenses. You may be able to do this quickly using online banking.

Subtract your debt obligations from Step 2 from your total income in Step 3 to see how much you have available for living expenses. Decide how much of your monthly income should be allocated to each spending category, and stick to your budget. Budget-tracking software can help you monitor your spending and stay on track.

Step 7: Look for Extra Money

Examine your budget for areas where you could reduce your spending, and find extra money to pay your debt obligations faster. See Chapter 15. Postpone a major purchase, such as a car, appliance, or vacation, and pay down your loan balance or credit card debt instead. Increase the amount going into your savings, and when it surpasses a specified amount, use the extra to pay off your debts. Sell something of value that you do not need any more. Look for ways to earn extra income.

Step 8: Establish a Pattern that will Increase your Prosperity

Make freedom from debt a priority. Develop a strategy for steadily paying off your student loans and other debt obligations while putting aside savings for emergencies and future expenses. Manage your loans and other debts efficiently so that your credit score improves and you can get lower interest rates. Periodically review your credit reports and refinance your debt when your credit score improves. Save up for a down payment on a house, car, or boat.

APPENDIX B

Glossary

529 Plan: A tax-deferred or tax-free investment account used to save money for education expenses.

Ability-to-Benefit Test (ATB): A test to determine whether a student applying for Title IV student financial aid who does not have a high-school diploma or its equivalent would be able to succeed in a college setting.

Academic Competitiveness Grant: A grant of up to $750 for qualified students in their first academic year and up to $1,300 for their second year of study.

Academic year: A one-year period, often from July 1 to June 30 of the next calendar year. A school that uses terms instead of semesters may count 30 weeks of instructional time as an academic year.

Accrued interest: Interest that accumulates on the unpaid principal balance of a loan; the amount of money that is repaid on a loan in addition to the original interest.

ACT Assessment: A national college admission examination that consists of tests in English, mathematics, reading, science, and writing.

Active Duty Student Deferment: A deferment granted to a student who leaves school for active military duty and intends to return and complete his or her education.

Active military service: Deployment to a battle zone or during a national emergency.

Adjusted Gross Income (AGI): Taxable income from all sources, calculated on the annual IRS tax return.

Administrative Cost Allowance (ACA): Money reimbursed by the federal government to a guaranty agency for administrative expenses involved in the operation of its program.

Advanced Placement (AP) Courses: College-level classes taken by students while they are still in high school.

ALL Student Loan: A large, non-profit education lender.

AmeriCorps: A U.S. national service program that gives education credits in exchange for a year of public service.

AmeriCorps Education Award (Segal AmeriCorps Education Award): An award of up to $4,725 that pays off qualified student loans or qualified education expenses for Ameri-Corps volunteers.

Anticipated Completion Date: The date on which the school expects the required curriculum to be completed.

Anticipated Separation Date: The date when a student borrower is expected to graduate or cease to attend classes more than half-time.

Award letter: A letter sent by a school financial aid office to a student detailing its offer of financial assistance, including scholarships, grants, and loans.

Balance: The amount that remains to be repaid on a loan.

Bankruptcy: A legal declaration that an individual is unable to pay his or her debts, usually resulting in some kind of debt relief.

BEOG: Basic Educational Opportunity Grant, now called a "Pell Grant."

Cohort default rate: The percentage of a school's borrowers who enter repayment on FFEL or Direct Loans during a particular federal fiscal year and default before three fiscal years have ended.

College Cost Reduction and Access Act of 2007 (CCRAA): Legislation that introduced income-based repayment (IBR) and public service loan forgiveness, as well as other reforms.

Consolidation loan: A single loan taken out to pay off multiple loans at a more favorable interest rate.

Constant dollar: An adjustment that uses the Consumer Price Indexes from various years to compare dollar values from one period to another.

Cost of Attendance: The estimated cost, as determined by a school, of attendance for one year, including tuition, fees, room and board, books, supplies, and incidental expenses.

Credit reporting agency: An agency that compiles data on each consumer's debt payment history and reports to banks and financial institutions.

Credit score: A numerical assessment of an individual's ability to repay a loan.

Debt snowball: A strategy for rapidly paying off credit card balances in which the monthly payment for one card is added to a second card when the first one is paid off.

Default: Failure to repay a loan.

Deferment: A temporary suspension of loan payments granted to borrowers in specific circumstances.

Deficit Reduction Act of 2005: A law that greatly reduced government subsidies for student loans.

Department of Education: The U.S. government agency that administers the student financial aid and loan program.

Direct Lending Schools: Schools that offer student loans through the Direct Loan program.

Direct Loan: A subsidized or unsubsidized federal loan administered directly through the school.

Discharge: The cancellation of all principal and interest owed on a loan.

DOE: The U.S. Department of Education.

Exit counseling: Education about loan repayment offered to a borrower at the time of leaving school.

Expected Family Contribution (EFC): A calculation of how much a student and the student's family are expected to pay out of pocket for an education.

Extended Repayment Plan: A repayment plan that lowers the amount of each monthly payment by extending the term of the loan.

FAFSA: Free Application for Federal Student Aid.

Federal Direct Consolidation Loan: A Direct Loan that refinances several individual government loans as a single loan with a lower interest rate.

Federal Family Education Loans (FFEL): A program in which loans are made by private lenders and subsidized and guaranteed by the federal government.

FFEL: Federal Family Education Loans.

FFEL consolidation loan: A single FFEL loan with a fixed interest rate taken out to pay off several student loans.

FICO: A formula used by the Fair Isaac Corporation to assign a numerical score indicating the likelihood that a borrower will repay a debt.

Forbearance: An agreement in which a lender allows a borrower to temporarily delay or reduce payments during a period of financial hardship.

Free Application for Federal Student Aid (FAFSA): An application that must be filled out by every student requesting financial aid for education.

Freedom of Information Act (FOIA) request: A request for access to personal information in the records of a federal agency.

Graduate Fellowship Deferment: A deferment that allows borrowers of federal student loans to delay payment while they pursue non-classroom graduate studies under a fellowship from a university.

Grant: Money given to a student to pay for education-related expenses.

Guarantor: A third party that guarantees to pay a lender the outstanding principal and interest of a student loan if the borrower defaults on the loan.

Health Education Assistance Loan (HEAL): A government program that insured educational loans made by private lenders to graduate students in the health professions between 1978 and 1998.

Health Resources and Services Administration (HRSA): A federal government agency that administers student loans for future health service workers.

Higher Education Act of 1965: A law that provides for the administration of federal higher education programs.

Income Contingent Repayment Plan (ICR): A student loan repayment plan that bases the amount of monthly payments on the borrower's annual income.

Interest capitalization cap: A limit placed on the amount of unpaid interest that can be capitalized (added to the loan balance).

Individual Retirement Account (IRA): A tax-deferred investment account to which an individual makes tax-deferred contributions for retirement savings.

Lender: A bank or institution that provides the funds for a student loan and receives the interest.

Loan forgiveness program: Program that forgives federal student loans for borrowers employed in specific occupations.

Loan forgiveness for service in areas of national need: A government program to forgive student loans of employees serving in certain areas of national need.

Loan Repayment for Civil Legal Assistance Attorneys: A proposed bill to provide government funds for loan forgiveness for civil legal assistance attorneys.

Loans for Disadvantaged Students: A program of long-term, low-interest loans for full-time students earning a degree in allopathic medicine, osteopathic medicine, dentistry, optometry, podiatric medicine, pharmacy, or veterinary medicine.

Master Promissory Note (MPN): A promissory note for Stafford or Perkins loans that is valid for ten years and covers multiple loans.

Military Deferment: A deferment given to members of the Armed Forces who are deployed on active duty during a war or national emergency.

National Service Trust: A U.S. Treasury account that pays education awards for public service programs such as AmeriCorps and SCA.

Net Present Value (NPV): A method for comparing the current value of money with its future value by accounting for the effect of inflation on future buying power, and the possible earnings if money available today is invested at market interest rates.

NDSL: National Direct Student Loan, now known as a "Perkins loan."

Nursing Student Loan program: A program that provides long-term, low-interest rate loans to full-time and half-time students of nursing.

Peer-to-peer loan: A loan made by one individual to another, formalized by a legal loan contract.

Pell Grant: A need-based federal grant to pay qualified education expenses.

Perkins Loans: Low-interest subsidized loans awarded by a school to undergraduate and graduate students with exceptional financial need.

PIN: Department of Education Personal Identification Number. A four-digit confidential ID number used to electronically sign the FAFSA and access personal loan information online.

PLUS loans: Parental Loan for Undergraduate Studies loans.

Public Service Loan Forgiveness Program: A program established in 2007 providing for $5,000 in loan forgiveness to be distributed over a five-year period to borrowers employed in low-paid public service jobs.

Primary Care Loan (PCL): A program that offers low cost federal loans for medical students who commit themselves to entering primary health care practice for a minimum period of time.

Prepaid College Tuition plan: A savings plan that allows families to lock in the current cost of tuition at a university by paying it in advance.

Principal: The original amount of a loan.

Promissory Note: The legal agreement between lender and borrower that specifies the terms of a loan in a signed document.

Public Service Loan Forgiveness Program: A federal program initiated in 2007 that forgives the balance of federal student loans after the borrower has been employed in public service for ten years.

Rehabilitation: The procedure for bringing a loan out of default and reinstituting a payment plan.

Rehabilitation Training Program Deferment: A temporary deferment that allows borrowers of federal student loans to delay payments while they are undergoing rehabilitation or physical therapy.

Scholarship: Money given to a student to pay for education.

Servicing agency: A third-party agency that administers loan payments and handles collections.

Student Aid Report (SAR): A report of a student's eligibility for financial aid, prepared by the Department of Education.

Sallie Mae: A student loan company created as a government enterprise in 1972 to administer federally-insured loans, and privatized in 2004.

Single holder rule: A rule repealed in 2005 that required borrowers whose loans were all from a single lender to consolidate with that lender.

Special Allowance Payment: A subsidy paid by the U.S. government to student lenders to make up the difference between market interest rates and the fixed rates on student loans.

Standard Repayment Plan: A student loan repayment plan under which you make a fixed monthly payment for a term of up to ten years.

Student Loan Marketing Association: Sallie Mae.

Subsidized student loan: A Stafford loan for which the government pays the interest while the student is in school and during periods of deferment.

Title IV: The portion of the Higher Education Act of 1965 that provides for the administration of federal student financial aid.

Unemployment Deferment: A temporary deferment that allows borrowers of federal student loans to delay payments while they are unemployed.

Unsubsidized student loan: A Stafford loan for which interest accrues during the time the student is in school and during deferment periods.

Weighted Average Interest Rate: A calculation used to determine the interest rate for consolidated loans that averages the interest rates of the individual loans according to the amount of each loan balance.

ABOUT THE AUTHOR

Martha Maeda is an economic historian and writes on politics, ethics and modern philosophy. After graduating from Northwestern University, she lived and worked in Australia, Japan, Latin America and several African countries, before settling in the United States. She has a special interest in micro-economics and in the effects of globalization on the lives and businesses of people all over the world.

BIBLIOGRAPHY

Berkner, Lutz K., Shirley He, Stephen Lew, Melissa Cominole, Peter Siegel, and James Griffith. *2003-04 National postsecondary student aid study (NPSAS:04): student financial aid estimates for 2003-04.* Washington, D.C.: U.S. Department of Education, National Center for Education Statistics. 2005.

Carey, Kevin. *A Matter of Degrees: Improving Graduation Rates in Four-year Colleges and Universities.* Washington D.C.: Education Trust. 2004. (**www2.edtrust.org/NR/rdonlyres/11B4283F-104E-4511-B0CA-1D3023231157/0/highered.pdf**)

CNN, Rising Costs Could Push College Out of Reach, CNN.com. December 3, 2008. (**www.cnn.com/2008/LIVING/personal/12/03/college.costs/index.html**) Accessed April 3, 2009.

College Board. "Federal Student Aid to Undergraduates Shows Slow Growth, While Published Tuition Prices Continue to Rise." College Board Press Release. October 22, 2007.

CollegeBoard. Trends in College Pricing 2008. Trends in Higher Education Series. College Board, 2008. (**http://professionals.collegeboard.com/profdownload/trends-in-college-pricing-2008.pdf**) Accessed April 3, 2009.

CollegeBoard. Trends in Student Aid 2008. Trends in Higher Education Series. College Board, 2008. (**http://professionals.collegeboard.com/profdownload/trends-in-student-aid-2008.pdf**) Accessed April 3, 2009.

DRBS, *Fundamentals of U.S. Structured Finance – ABS 2008 Year in Review and Outlook for 2009*, February 2009. (**www.dbrs.com/research/226477/fundamentals-of-u-s-structured-finance-abs-2008-year-in-review-and-outlook-for-2009.pdf**) Accessed April 3, 2009.

Hess, Frederick M. *Footing the Tuition Bill: The New Student Loan Sector*. Washington, D.C.: AEI Press. 2007.

Khalfani-Cox, L. *Zero Debt for College Grads: From Student Loans to Financial Freedom*. New York, Kaplan Pub. 2007.

Knapp, Laura G., Janice E. Kelly-Reid, Scott A. Ginder, and Elise S. Miller. 2008. *Enrollment in Postsecondary Institutions, Fall 2006; Graduation Rates, 2000 & 2003 Cohorts; and Financial Statistics, Fiscal Year 2006*. First Look. NCES 2008-173. National Center for Education Statistics. Available from: ED Pubs. P.O. Box 1398, Jessup, MD 20794-1398. Tel: 877-433-7827; Web site: (**http://nces.ed.gov/help/orderinfo.asp**). Accessed April 3, 2009

Mitchell, Nancy. 2006. Surviving Your Student Loans. [S.l.]: Booklocker.com, Inc. ISBN 159113837X 9781591138372

Mundis, Jerrold J. *How to Get out of Debt, Stay out of Debt & Live Prosperously*. Toronto: Bantam Books. 1988.

Nellie Mae. *Undergraduate Students and Credit Cards in 2004: An Analysis of Usage Rates and Trends. NellieMae.com.* May, 2005. (**www.nelliemae.com/library/research_12.html**) Accessed April 3, 2009.

Nellie Mae. *Graduate Students and Credit Cards Fall 2006.* **NellieMae. com**. August, 2007. (**www.nelliemae.com/pdf/ccstudy_2006.pdf**) Accessed April 3, 2009.

Project on Student Debt. *Student Debt and the Class of 2007... Average Debt by State, Sector, and School.* [Berkeley, CA.]: Project on Student Debt. 2006. (**http://projectonstudentdebt.org/files/pub/classof2007.pdf**) Accessed April 3, 2009.

Sallie Mae, *Sallie Mae announces fourth-quarter and full-year 2007 results.* **SallieMae.com**. January, 2008. (**www.salliemae.com/about/news_info/newsreleases/012308.htm**) Accessed April 3, 2009

Sutton, Garrett. *The ABC's of Getting out of Debt: Turn Bad Debt into Good Debt and Bad Credit into Good Credit.* New York: Warner Books. 2004.

The Education Trust. Empty Caps and Gowns: New analysis reveals deep problems in the graduation rates at four-year colleges and universities, but finds that some institutions do a much better job graduating their students than others. The Education Trust. May 26, 2004. (**http://www2.edtrust.org/EdTrust/Press+Room/higher+ed+report.htm**)

Ventura, John. **Managing Debt for Dummies**. For Dummies. Hoboken, N.J.: Wiley. 2007.

INDEX